THE FAITH OF THE CHURCH

THE CHURCH'S TEACHING

In Preparation

VOLUME THREE

The Faith
of the Church

JAMES A. PIKE and
W. NORMAN PITTENGER

*With the editorial collaboration of Arthur C.
Lichtenberger, D.D., and with the assistance of
the Authors' Committee of the Department of
Christian Education of The Protestant Episcopal
Church*

THE
Seabury Press

GREENWICH · CONNECTICUT

SIXTH PRINTING MARCH, 1956

Contents

Foreword

THIS book is the third volume in THE CHURCH'S TEACHING series. Because it is about *The Faith of the Church* it is by far the most crucial book in the series. It has not been an easy book to write. The Authors' Committee has labored over it for three and a half years. The co-authors have rewritten not one but all its chapters time and time again. Critics of every shade of churchmanship have patiently read manuscript and generously helped with a host of useful suggestions. If ever a book produced for the Church was a labor of patience and love, it is this volume. Whatever faults it may prove to have, one of them will not be that it was hastily conceived or rapidly thrown together.

This book is written not as if we were discussing a set of theological propositions, but from *within* the living community of the Church. Hence it begins with a proclamation of those mighty acts by which God has saved the world. This proclamation is conveniently summarized in the Creeds, and these form the framework for this book.

The Creeds as statements never can take the place of

faith in God and response in trust, to his saving work. Anglicanism always has clearly understood that the Christian way is a way of redeemed relationship with God. Our theology is therefore that of a living community of believing people who are members of the Body of Christ; our life is a life-in-a-faith-relationship, made possible by the Christian proclamation, based on Scripture, summed up in the Creeds, expressed in worship, and above all, manifest in life.

It is with this clearly in mind that we have tried to write a book on *The Faith of the Church*.

JOHN HEUSS
V. O. WARD

Preface

IN this book we have sought to state as directly and plainly as possible the elements of the Christian faith "as this Church hath received the same" and as this faith is expressed in *The Book of Common Prayer*. This book does not represent favorite ideas of its authors; it attempts to express the common beliefs of those who belong to the Anglican Communion, especially as found in our own land, in the Episcopal Church.

Of course there are different emphases within our communion. This we all know. Some people regret the fact; we rejoice in it. The reason for our rejoicing in this variety of emphasis is that it helps to vindicate the claim which we like to make, that the Anglican Church is "the roomiest Church in Christendom." It is roomy, not because it does not care about what people believe, but because it knows that the truth of the Christian Gospel is so wonderfully rich and so infinitely great that no single human expression can exhaust all its truth and splendor. It is the claim of the Episcopal Church that it is *Catholic* in its maintenance of the historic faith and worship and order. It is *Protestant* in that it sees its teaching and practice under the judgment of God, and through continuing reformation has freed itself from distortions of Catholic faith and order which arose in the Middle Ages and have arisen since. It welcomes new truth, new insight, the contributions of scientific and secular thought, with the certain confidence that all truth is God's truth.

We have organized the book around the articles of the Christian Creeds, treating them less as definitions than as windows through which the faith may be seen—truly symbols, which is one ancient name for the Creeds.

The experience of writing this book has demonstrated beyond shadow of doubt the essential agreement of us all in the essential things of our faith. Thanks to the coöperation of the other members of the Authors' Committee, whose names appear on another page, and because of the ready helpfulness of many critics, we have been enabled to share in our task with representatives of every school of thought within the Church. Much of what is found in this book is not our own, but the contribution of those who have helped us in this fashion. To that which we have written, these collaborators almost invariably have given their cordial assent; where there has been difference of opinion, we have worked out with their help a statement which has met almost universal agreement. It is for this reason that we are bold to say that the Church is much more at one, much more in agreement, much more a family at unity with itself than some have assumed.

Furthermore, our labor has had an unexpectedly valuable ecumenical result. For we have ventured to have this book read, in manuscript, by members of other Christian

4

bodies; and we have been reassured to find that, apart from the emphases which are uniquely Anglican, the faith which we state here is not peculiarly our own but is common to "all who profess and call themselves Christians," and even the statement of those matters which are more distinctively Anglican has received sympathetic and interested response. Thus it is our hope that this undertaking will prove to be a genuine contribution to the growth of true ecumenical understanding.

It remains only to say that we are grateful to all who have helped with this book, both on the Authors' Committee and amongst our first readers and critics. Of considerable help in the planning of the work was a meeting of an informal group which included, in addition to members of the Authors' Committee, the Rt. Rev. Angus Dun, D.D., Bishop of Washington; the Rev. John V. Butler, D.D., rector of Trinity Church, Princeton, N. J.; and the Rev. William J. Wolf, TH.D., professor in the Episcopal Theological School. We are grateful to the Rev. Frederick Q. Shafer, chairman of the Department of Religion, University of the South, for a draft which contributed substantially to Chapter IV, and to the Rev. Albert T. Mollegen, D.D., of the Virginia Theological Seminary, who drafted a section of Chapter XI. We wish to note also the assistance rendered by Miss Ruth Garland in the technical preparation of the bibliography and the index. Above all, we are indebted to the Rt. Rev. Arthur C. Lichtenberger, D.D., S.T.D., Bishop Coadjutor of Missouri, who while a professor at the General Theological Seminary gave generously of his time in the task of editorial revision, so that the styles of the undersigned authors might not be too blatantly contrasted.

We hope and pray that these pages may do a useful work in helping our people witness in life and in doctrine to "the faith which was once for all delivered to the saints."

JAMES A. PIKE
W. NORMAN PITTENGER

New York, N. Y.
Whitsuntide, 1951

The Christian Gospel

Two thousand years ago a small band of men went out into the streets of Jerusalem, and into dozens of other towns and cities of the Graeco-Roman world, and proclaimed the Christian Gospel: the good news of salvation. They were fearless in their proclamation; they were on fire with their message. They had a story to tell, and they told it without faltering, conscious that power not their own enabled them to speak out bravely. The story they told was that God had done something new, something which changed everything, something which turned the world upside down. What was the story?

The New Testament in the second chapter of the Acts of the Apostles records the story as proclaimed by the early Christians. On the day of Pentecost the disciples of Jesus were gathered together *with one accord in one place*. They were filled with the Holy Spirit, who took possession of them and sent them out to proclaim the good news.

7

Here is the first Christian sermon, preached by St. Peter. "This zeal and enthusiasm which you see," to paraphrase his words, "has come because the promises made to the Old Testament prophets are being fulfilled. God has sent his Spirit upon us, so that we may preach the mighty working by which he has redeemed the world. You know of Jesus of Nazareth, whom your rulers crucified. That same Jesus, who was sent forth from God and approved among you by the signs which He performed, has now by God's mighty act been raised from the dead. Because He is risen, He has shed forth the Holy Spirit; and in the power of the Spirit, we are sent out to call men to repentance and to acceptance of Jesus as Lord of men and redeemer of the world."

On another occasion (*Acts 5:30-32*) the same apostle boldly declared: *The God of our fathers raised up Jesus, whom ye slew and hanged on a tree. Him God hath exalted with his right hand to be a Prince and a Saviour, for to give repentance to Israel, and forgiveness of sins. And we are his witnesses . . .*

Again, St. Peter says of Jesus that God anointed Him *with the Holy Ghost and with power: who went about doing good, and healing all that were oppressed of the devil; for God was with him. And we are witnesses of all things which he did both in the land of the Jews, and in Jerusalem; whom they slew and hanged on a tree. Him God raised up the third day, and shewed him openly . . . and he commanded us to preach unto the people, and to testify that it is he which was ordained of God to be the judge of quick and dead. To him give all the prophets witness, that through his name whosoever believeth in him shall receive remission of sins* (*Acts 10:38-43*).

This, then, is the earliest preaching of the Good News.

8

It was not so much information about God's nature as proclamation of God's act. It was the affirmation that God had done something new and wonderful: he had acted in and through Jesus of Nazareth, so that *whosoever believeth in him shall receive remission of sins*. Life received a new meaning, men were empowered from on high, a new creation was established by God's deed. This was the Gospel: that in Jesus *God hath visited and redeemed his people*.

This was the story which the Christian missionaries told as they traveled about the Mediterranean. This was the apostolic preaching. As it finally reached a more or less stable form, it ran like this: "The promised age has dawned, the prophecies are fulfilled. Jesus of Nazareth has come in the power of the Spirit, wrought mighty works and taught with authority. He has been crucified, was dead, and was buried. But the third day, He rose again from the dead; now He is exalted at God's right hand as Lord and Christ. He will come again in glory. Meanwhile, the company of those who believe in Him is marked off as the new Israel of God, uniquely His people, by the gift of the Holy Spirit. In His name forgiveness and salvation are offered to men. Therefore, we call upon you to repent and believe." [1]

The letters of St. Paul are entirely based on this theme, which the apostle approaches and states in many different ways. The first four books of the New Testament are called gospels, because they tell this story of good news: the word *gospel* in Greek means good news. St. Mark, for example, informs us that he tells the story of Jesus' earthly ministry as *the beginning of the gospel of Jesus Christ, the Son of God*. St. John's Gospel is written that *ye might believe that*

---

[1] C. Harold Dodd, *History and the Gospel,* page 72.

9

Jesus is the Christ, the Son of God; and that believing ye might have life through his name. The last book of the New Testament, the Revelation of St. John the Divine, is in essence a declaration that Jesus who came by God's act, will come again to judge the world, vindicating His sovereign rule over men and nature.

Furthermore, the beginnings of theological development are already seen in the New Testament itself. In St. Paul's letters, for example, we can trace the attempts of the great apostle to find language adequate to express all that the primitive *kerygma*[2] meant. If Christ is indeed the Messiah of God, acting on God's behalf, He must be the agent of God in redemption. And if He is that, He must be so much God's expression that it is impossible to conceive of the world, or its creation, without taking Him into account. Thus He is seen to be none other than *the Word of God,* as St. John phrases it in his gospel (*St. John 1:1-16*), *without whom nothing was made, who was in the beginning with God,* who, indeed, *is God.* The reader should study especially St. Paul's Epistles to the Philippians and the Colossians, and St. John's Gospel, to note the way in which such inevitable development took place within the first few decades after the Resurrection.

THE KERYGMA AND THE CREEDS

A LITTLE thought will make it clear that this primitive preaching or *kerygma,* with the development just noted, is the same fundamentally as that summary of the Christian faith which is stated in the earliest of the creeds. The Apostles' Creed, the historical development of which has been described in the preceding volume,[3] is but an ex-

---

[2] The Greek word used to describe *the preaching* in the New Testament.
[3] *Chapters in Church History,* Chapter I.

pansion of the earliest Christian message. It is a fuller and more dramatic way of stating what St. Peter said in the words quoted above.

I believe in God the Father Almighty, Maker of heaven and earth:
And in Jesus Christ his only Son our Lord:
Who was conceived by the Holy Ghost, Born of the Virgin Mary:
Suffered under Pontius Pilate, Was crucified, dead, and buried:
He descended into hell; The third day he rose again from the dead: He ascended into heaven, And sitteth on the right hand of God the Father Almighty:
From thence he shall come to judge the quick and the dead.
I believe in the Holy Ghost: The holy Catholic Church; the Communion of Saints: The Forgiveness of sins: The resurrection of the body: And the Life everlasting. Amen.

These phrases, some of them dating from the second century, were first employed in approximately their present form by Christians when they were made members of the Church in baptism. They were their pledge of allegiance to the Christian faith.

The longer Nicene Creed is another expansion of the same primitive Christian preaching, new clauses of a more theological nature having been introduced for the purpose of excluding the errors of those who denied the great affirmations of the Gospel. The fundamentals which the Church had held from the beginning to be the very heart of its unique message to the world, and the reason for the Church's existence, were thus more clearly stated and were protected from serious misinterpretation. In the form which appears in our Prayer Book, this creed runs:

I believe in one God the Father Almighty, Maker of heaven and earth,

And of all things visible and invisible:

And in one Lord Jesus Christ, the only-begotten Son of God;

Begotten of his Father before all worlds,

God of God, Light of Light, Very God of very God;

Begotten, not made;

Being of one substance with the Father;

By whom all things were made:[4]

Who for us men and for our salvation came down from heaven,

And was incarnate by the Holy Ghost of the Virgin Mary,

And was made man:

And was crucified also for us under Pontius Pilate;

He suffered and was buried:

And the third day he rose again according to the Scriptures:

And ascended into heaven, And sitteth on the right hand of the Father:

And he shall come again, with glory, to judge both the quick and the dead;

Whose kingdom shall have no end.

And I believe in the Holy Ghost, The Lord, and Giver of Life,

Who proceedeth from the Father and the Son;[5]

---

[4] The literal translation of the Greek original is "*through* whom all things were made."

[5] The original form of the creed omitted the phrase *and the Son.* It was inserted much later in the Western Church.

*Who with the Father and the Son together is worshipped
and glorified;*
Who spake by the Prophets:
And I believe one Catholic and Apostolic Church:[6]
I acknowledge one Baptism for the remission of sins:
And I look for the Resurrection of the dead:
And the Life of the world to come. Amen.

So Christianity went out from its Jewish homeland, built upon this apostolic faith, and won thousands to its way of life. First came the Gospel, proclaimed by the Church through its evangelists; in consequence of that Gospel, men found their lives transfigured and themselves "new creatures in Christ Jesus." As a result, a new energy was released into the Roman Empire which transformed the entire Western world.

The Christians were sure of their creed. They found the center of their common life in the Common Meal—the Holy Communion. They lived in fellowship with one another in Christ. They became, as one writer put it, "a third race." They were neither Jews nor Greeks, in first loyalties, but Christians, *a peculiar people, a royal priesthood* (*I Peter 2:9*) who were as leaven in the world, as light in the darkness. But because the Christians, like all other human beings, lived in the world of men and affairs, and above all because of their pagan environment, they were obliged to think about their faith. They were obliged to relate it to the rest of their experience. Theological development was bound to take place and did in fact take place immediately.

---

[6] The adjective *holy* is found in the original of the creed and was omitted by Cranmer in his translation by a mistake in historical knowledge.

THE purpose of this theological development, as *Chapters in Church History* has made clear, was primarily to assert the truth of Christ's redemption and to safeguard the Christian proclamation from various false theories, *heresies,* as they are called, which would have imperiled and perhaps destroyed the meaning of the story of God's mighty act in Christ. Thus it came about that certain *dogmas,* or permanently necessary Christian assertions, were made by the Church.[7] They were advanced and accepted not because of a desire to engage in speculation of a philosophical or theoretical nature, but because of the necessity for affirming the full truth of the Christian Gospel in all its integrity. Modern men are used to the idea of the *data* or the *given* in scientific research. Dogma is also *given.* The Church does not foist dogmas on us, in an arbitrary and dictatorial manner. It presents them as essential because it sees that they are statements of the very stuff of Christian faith. The Church itself could not set them aside without altering its own character as bearer of the Christian revelation. In later chapters these central dogmas will be considered in detail: the Incarnation, the Atonement, and the Trinity, for example. Each of them safeguards essential elements in *the faith once delivered to the saints (Jude 1:3).* Their sole purpose is to maintain in its fullness the

---

[7] The term *dogma* is here used to describe the central affirmations of the Christian faith as these are given in the Scriptures and in the Creeds. Some of the dogmas (*e.g.* the Incarnation) have been ecclesiastically defined at the so-called ecumenical councils; others have never received a similar precise definition but are nevertheless to be regarded as of the essence of the faith (*e.g.* the Creation and the Atonement). Secondary to these dogmas are doctrinal speculations as to how these are to be interpreted. The present usage of these terms is chosen for convenience' sake, and is not always so employed in theological textbooks.

14

truth about God's redemptive act which is at the center of the Church's continuing life in faith.

The dogma of the Incarnation, for example, guarantees the crucial Christian belief in our Lord Jesus Christ. If Christ is not truly God of God, then the preaching about Him is only information about what a great man once did. There remains only the humanism by which man must save himself, if he is ever to be saved. If Christ is not truly man, the Gospel is not brought to bear directly upon human life and its need. We are once more without empowering from God, given to us in terms that we can understand and use. If in Christ, God and man are not uniquely and eternally one, so that He is truly both our God and our Brother, then His life may be but a passing incident, with no enduring meaning for all men everywhere and at all times. Each one of these possibilities destroys the Gospel and by so doing leaves men unredeemed. Christian dogma, as this illustration shows, is rooted in the Christian Gospel and illuminates that Gospel's meaning.

But, of course, speculative systems of doctrine are not in the same category as Christian dogma. In every age, men are bound to work out a system in which the gospel by which they live is related to the thought-forms, the particular needs, the climate of opinion, which are then prevalent. The great systematic theologians of the Church have performed this indispensable task from Clement of Alexandria, Origen, and Augustine, through Thomas Aquinas, Luther, and Calvin, down to our own day. The validity of these various systems is determined by their loyalty to the Gospel. This means by their loyalty to the Holy Scriptures which record the acts of God upon which the creeds are based. Furthermore, the validity of these systems is determined by the degree to which they maintain and safeguard such dogmas as the Incarnation and the Trinity.

THE ANGLICAN WAY

WHILE we must always be grateful for the several systems, we must never confuse them with the central dogmas of the faith itself. It is these alone which safeguard the life in faith which the Church knows and cherishes. Anglicanism[8] has no official theologian in its history. Hence it can welcome contributions from any system but it finds absolute authority in none. It may learn from Augustine and Aquinas, and from Luther and Calvin, but it is not bound to any of them. It gives allegiance simply to the Apostles' Creed and the Nicene Creed; and through these, to the central Christian dogmas which the Creeds express. Above all, it is bound to Holy Scripture itself for the Bible is "the Word of God." [9] In it is the record of God's revelation in Christ, the story of what God did, out of which the Gospel comes. The Old Testament prepares for the New. The New Testament fulfills the Old. And both together are the great oratorio of divine redemption which the Christian Church knows and loves. Every credal statement is to be believed insofar as it may be proved (that is, tested) by an appeal to Scripture.[10] The Anglican Communion does not intend to preclude development nor deny the right use of the human reason. It does insist, however,

---

[8] This word is used to describe all the Churches, throughout the world, which are in communion with the Archbishop of Canterbury and owe their historic origin to the mother Church of England. There are some forty million Anglicans living in every continent in the world, among them two million American Episcopalians.

[9] See *The Holy Scriptures,* pages 9-10.

[10] Articles of Religion, Article VIII.

16

that nothing can be taught by the Church as necessary to salvation which is not contained in the Holy Scriptures. This is the test of sound development. Here is the evangelical emphasis which is necessary to safeguard the Catholic tradition, of which it is a part, from wild imaginings and erroneous teaching.[11]

The special quality or genius of the Anglican Communion, in matters of faith, may be discovered right here. The English Reformers were very clear about the appeal to history.[12] They insisted that the basis for the Christian faith is in the saving acts of God, recorded in Holy Scripture. That is what they meant by the necessity for proving. But they were equally concerned to emphasize that the ancient Fathers of the Church provided an invaluable clue to the kind of interpretation of the Scriptures which is sound and accurate; a norm by which later interpretation of the Scriptures could be judged. And this insistence of the English Reformers involved them, of necessity, in a recognition of two other factors: the place of religious experience and the value of reason.

If we are to appeal to Scripture and to the interpretation given by the Fathers of the Church during the first four centuries of Christian faith, we must use our mind. We dare not claim that our minds can give us any infallible truth, but we must give thoughtful study and careful reasoning to the religious as to every other realm of experience. At the same time, we must recognize that one of the tests of truth, although by no means the only one, is fruitfulness in living. If a belief enriches and deepens our experience, we can assert that it has a claim to contain truth.

---

[11] See the account of the meaning of the English Reformation in *Chapters in Church History*, pages 151-177.
[12] See *Chapters in Church History*, Chapter IV.

If, for example, the quality of life which we affirm to be Christian is nourished and strengthened by such a dogma as the Incarnation, there is good reason for holding fast to that dogma. If that dogma makes more sense of the world in which we live, it has an even weightier claim.

All this is important, yet it has its dangers. Christianity is not content to appeal to religious experience alone, for it is an historical faith. Hence we are obliged to say that if, in addition to these other tests and to the witness of the Fathers, it also can be seen that the Incarnation is plainly stated or implied in the account of God's work as reported in Scripture, we shall then, and then only, be prepared without hesitation to assert it as necessary to salvation. But there may be beliefs which are so contrary to the essential message of the Gospel, or so irrelevant to its major emphases, that they must be regarded as dangerous or unessential, no matter how helpful some may think them to be. This is the reason that Anglican theologians have contended that certain recent Roman Catholic dogmatic pronouncements are erroneous.[13]

This kind of approach to the faith is the peculiar *ethos* or determining spirit of the Anglican Communion. It is not so much the statement of particular truths as it is a way of understanding and evaluating all truth. It implies no false absolutism; but it does recognize the rightful place of authority. The great theologians of the Anglican Communion, in different ways and with varying emphases, have all been marked by this firm yet reasonable spirit. The

---

[13] Examples of these are provided by the promulgation, as required for saving faith, of the Immaculate Conception of the Virgin Mary (1854); the Infallibility of the Pope (1870); and, most recently, the Bodily Assumption of the Virgin (1950). For none of these is there scriptural evidence and it cannot even be claimed that they are supported by the primitive and very early Christian Church.

Anglican *ethos* is an evangelical Catholicism, a living orthodoxy.

SCRIPTURE AND TRADITION

It is in accord with this *ethos* that Anglicanism has asserted that there is an essential place for tradition in the Christian religion. This tradition is not set alongside the Scriptures which contain the Word of God. It is a tradition which is grounded in and nourished by the Scriptures. In a sense, indeed, the Scriptures themselves are tradition, in that they are handed down from generation to generation by the believing community. The act of God which created that community gave to it the Scriptures. Within the community they were set down in written form, or (in the case of the Old Testament) taken over from the older Israel as the preparation for the Gospel. They show what the Christian Gospel was in its first days and how that Gospel spread into the world. They have a classical and normative significance. But there is also in the tradition, in this wide sense, a wealth of other material in addition to, and dependent on, the Scriptures.

The hymns of the Church, for example, are a precious part of this living heritage. So are the liturgies or services of worship, passed down and hallowed through centuries of loving use. There are books of private devotion, the lives of the saints remembered and recounted, the writings of "doctors and confessors" (that is, the work of theologians in past ages); there are the Christian martyrs and their stories, and the simple account of holy and humble men of heart who have lived in the Church and for Christ. All this is part of the living community of faith today. We do not live only in the present but also in the past, building on the lives of those who have gone before us and who now rest in peace with the sign of faith.

Those who believe that Christianity is indeed the true religion, based on the mighty acts of God, cannot doubt that the guidance of the Holy Spirit has been with the Church in its development. Above all, He has been with the Church as it came to learn more deeply the meaning of its Gospel. The Holy Spirit does not work, necessarily, in ways that cut across normal human thinking, although sometimes He may. Certainly in the development of the primitive preaching into the Apostles' and Nicene Creeds and Christian dogma, His work has more surely been one of guidance, enlightening the minds of men to see into the things of Christ and inspiring them to state, in succinct fashion, the fundamental truths of the Gospel. There was nothing automatic here. It was the long, slow, careful growth of Christian understanding, as earnest and intelligent men sought to grasp the true meaning of that by which they lived.

THE LANGUAGE OF THE CREEDS

WHAT, then, of the language of the Creeds? How are we to regard them today?

Recall that Christianity was first preached as the *kerygma,* the proclamation of what God had done in and by Christ. He had entered with saving power into history, where men live, to redeem them from sin and open to them a life empowered by His Holy Spirit. This affirmation is concerned with the presence and action of eternity in time, God at work in the finite and temporal world. It was inevitable, therefore, that when the primitive preaching was summarized in the apostolic Creed, it should have been stated in language that had a symbolic quality. After all, we do not have first-hand knowledge of eternity, nor do we possess words which could express literally all that is involved in the Christian epic. The word *epic* is used purposely, since the Christian proclamation is a tale, the portrayal of God's ways with men. As it first comes to us, it is not a number of ideas, of propositions such as we might use to describe a set of philosophical principles, nor is it a collection of human opinions. It is a drama concerned with what God has wrought.

This may be illustrated by taking some words and phrases from the Apostles' Creed. For instance, the Creed describes God by the words *Father Almighty*. The first of these words, *Father,* is drawn from ordinary human experience, but when it is applied to God, it is clear that the word has a much deeper meaning than when applied to a human parent. The second word, *Almighty,* is also taken from human experience, yet when God is called *almighty* the term does not mean that God is a dictator who can and will arbitrarily do what He pleases.

Or again, when we say that Jesus Christ our Lord sits *at the right hand of the Father,* we do not mean that God literally has a right hand, nor that Jesus is actually sitting there. The phrase describes, in language drawn from human experience, "the highest place that heaven affords." Furthermore, when in the Nicene Creed we say that Christ *came down from heaven,* we do not mean that He descended from somewhere in the sky down to earth. We are declaring, with St. Irenaeus, that "He who is altogether divine" shared our human lot and was by His own will made "altogether human." Much creedal language partakes of this symbolic quality.

But to use the words symbol and symbolic is not to assert that the Creeds are untrue. Rather it is to say that there are great areas of experience which can best be described in words that have a pictorial and dramatic nature. When a man tells a woman that he loves her with all his heart, he is not referring to a certain portion of his circulatory system; he is using a picture-word to say that his affection is centered in the woman of his choice. Truth stated in literal words often falls far short of doing justice to that which is really intended. This is especially true of the deep and ultimate things of existence. The Creeds recognize this fact.

On the other hand, there can be no doubt that the Creeds are based upon historical events. That Jesus Christ our Lord was born as man, that He lived among us, that He died under Pontius Pilate, that He overcame death—here, all Christians believe, are indubitable historical facts which can never be shaken. The Christian religion, whatever else it may be, is an historical religion. Its Creeds anchor it to historical fact, thereby safeguarding it from all attempts to turn the faith into a theory or a speculation. And this essential historical basis, stated in the Creeds, is guaranteed by the appeal to Holy Scripture, where *that which was from the beginning, which we have heard, which we have seen with our eyes, which we have looked upon, and our hands have handled, of the Word of life (I John 1:1)* is plainly declared.

WHAT THE CREEDS AFFIRM

THE central Christian dogmas, like the Incarnation, the Atonement, and the Trinity, are to be seen then as the best, simplest, most satisfactory way of stating the significance which the Church found in the events upon which the Creeds are based. And when we affirm the Creeds, we are at the same time affirming the dogmas which they contain. When we learn about the dogmas, we are learning to see, with the eyes of Christian thought and experience, the innermost meaning and truth implicit in God's actions in history. Thus we are saved from intellectualism on the one hand, and from thoughtless credulity on the other. Our faith is our total self-commitment in trust and confidence to the God who in Christ has been made man, for us men and for our salvation. What used to be called our credal subscription is the way in which we affirm this fact of self-commitment in language made holy by centuries of use within the rich life of the Christian community.

There are those who say we should have a new creed expressed in words and ideas of our own day. But we are in no position, in a divided Christendom, to attempt any such thing. Even if we were, this suggestion really misses the point. A creed expressed in the words and ideas of our own day would be subject to constant alteration as our information about the world changed and new discoveries came to light. The historic Creeds are quite different. They are historically grounded and traditionally hallowed affirmations of the Christian belief of all ages. By the very fact that many of their words are pictorial or dramatic in nature, they deliver us from literalism. By their very antiquity, they unite us with our brethren in faith through all the ages of Christianity. Above all, by their close relationship to the primitive Christian proclamation, they ground us in the faith which is found in the pages of the New Testament and which informed the life of the earliest Christian believers. They are indeed indispensable.

Of course neither the Creeds nor the central dogmas of Christianity give us scientific information. Nor do they deal with philosophical ideas. They do not answer all the questions we might ask about the world. That is not their purpose. Christianity is not a philosophy. It is a faith. It does not offer men a metaphysic. It gives them a Gospel. Therefore its Creeds must be understood in that sense. They tell us what we need for our salvation; that is, what we must know about God and his ways with men, so that we can live with dignity and purpose here in this world, and have the assurance of life eternal.

Their proper setting is in the Church's worship. This is demonstrated by the fact that the Nicene and the Apostles' Creeds are normally used in the Holy Communion, and in Morning and Evening Prayer. Christians gather together to worship God through Christ by virtue of His revelation and redemption and in that setting they fitly profess their common belief. And Christian action, which flows from our life in Christ in His Body the Church, is the direct expression of the reality which we affirm when we stand and say, *I believe*. For if I believe thus, I must act thus. If I believe that God's mighty act is Christ, I must let Christ work His will in me. Faith, worship, and life are knit together in an indestructible whole.

CHRISTIAN BELIEF AND CHRISTIAN LIFE

THE Christian Creed cannot be understood apart from the Christian Church. The Creed is the expression of the Church's faith. And it is by that faith that the Church lives. We often ask what reason for being has this, that, or the other institution or society? In the Christian Church the reason for being of the community is stated in the Creed:

24

"This is why we are. We are like this, we say and do these things, because God himself has acted in history to save us. Because God has brought into existence this new creation in which Christ is Lord and where all who believe in Him live in newness of life. This is the Gospel we preach, because this is the only Gospel we know."

Thus in order to understand the Christian Church, we must understand and accept the Christian Creed. But conversely, in order to understand and accept the Christian Creed, we must share in the life and experience of the Christian Church. Those who remain on the outside will never be able to grasp what the Church means when it speaks of redemption in Christ, although they are perishing without that redemption. When men face the inexorable demand which the Christian Church makes upon them, and are prepared to say that they will commit themselves to the God who is proclaimed and to the Church which proclaims him, the affirmations in the Creed begin to come alive and to make sense. This is why it is correct to say that the Church itself is part of its Gospel, for it is the arena where the Gospel is both preached and known.

But to every one of us there comes the question, What does it mean to say, *I believe*? What is the nature of faith, by which we come to accept the faith? We have reviewed the earliest Christian proclamation and have discovered that it is the same Gospel that is preached today. We have seen that the living community of Christians, called the One Holy Catholic and Apostolic Church, is the same community as that which went forth two thousand years ago, to proclaim this Good News. But how about each one of us? How do we come to believe? What does it mean to stand up and say, *I believe in God the Father Almighty . . . ?*

I Believe in . . .

Hₒw do we come to believe? Some of us believe because we always have done so, because we were taught to, because we have repeatedly said the words of the Creed, and its affirmations are deeply rooted in our lives. Indeed, these great declarations have had a large part in making us what we are. But today more and more people are growing up without having been taught to believe. Many of them have never recited the words of the Creed, nor have they heard the story it tells. But fortunately it is also a fact that in these days more and more people are becoming aware that their hearts are empty because the world has no meaning for them. They find themselves looking at the Christian story as something which may provide meaning for life. This possibility is becoming an actuality. There are distinguished men of letters and science, and many plain people, who have come to say with all their hearts, *I believe in . . .*

To be sure, there is a danger of pride in the convert.

Sometimes he assumes that only those who have become Christian after mature decision really have the faith. There are those who have been in the Church from childhood and who have grown in grace as they have grown in years. The Church always has been concerned with them, to nurture them in the faith, to make and keep their commitment conscious and genuine at each stage of development, just as the Church always has been concerned to proclaim judgment and salvation to those still needing conversion.

HOW ONE COMES TO BELIEVE

YET it is the coming to faith of the converts that occupies the most vivid pages of the Christian tradition. St. Paul, St. Augustine, St. Francis, Martin Luther, and John Wesley are famous instances. This is because their adult religious experiences display so clearly the real nature of faith. They experience in a single crisis the whole process which in many a once-born saint has been too gradual to analyze. And so for this chapter, the *I believe* of the adult convert will be more useful for our study than the *I believe* of the everyday Christian of life-long loyalty.

How does the atheist or agnostic come to the faith of the Church? It is often assumed that such a one has weighed the arguments, has found that the articles of the Creed can be proved and that his mind has compelled him to become a Christian. The most obvious difficulty in such an assumption is that there are many intelligent and rational people who are not Christians. A deeper difficulty is in the very nature of the reasoning process itself.

Any geometry student will remember that axiom precedes theorem. It is not possible to start reasoning without assumptions. It is, for example, a theorem of geometry that the sum of two sides of a triangle is always greater than the other side. This rests on the axiom that a straight line is the shortest distance between two points. Such an axiom cannot be proved. We call axioms self-evident. But they are taken on faith. One cannot prove them. They are where one starts one's proving. The physicist, no less than the mathematician, starts with faith and then he reasons. He assumes, for example, that there is a world outside his mind —a sensible assumption to be sure, but one there is no way of proving. He assumes that what he finds will work in his laboratory today, will work tomorrow also. Were it not for his faith in these two things, his effort would hardly be worth the time. And it is plain that the nearer one gets to the final answer to the meaning of things, the more that answer must be received on faith if it is to be received at all.

Now God is the final Answer, the Ultimate Reality. If we could prove His existence it would be because from the standpoint of something more final we reasoned our way to Him. But then He would not be final, and thus not God. That which we assumed as more final would be God and we would have the same problem all over again. The existence of God cannot be demonstrated by logic or reason. But the many efforts to do so have been valuable in two ways:

They have shown that faith in God provides a more adequate understanding of reality than any alternative faith does; and

They have contributed much to the clarification of our thoughts about God.

THE NATURE OF FAITH

At this point a sincere and thoughtful man might answer, "If this is so I must remain an agnostic: I can't know, and

I can't accept things on faith." But the answer is: You do accept things on faith. You are living a certain way, you have a particular scale of values, you go about from day to day with definite assumptions. If you style yourself a humanist, you think and live as though man were the most significant reality in the world. If you are right, you are so by faith, not because you can prove that man is the most significant reality or even that he is valuable at all. If you style yourself a materialist, you assume that only physical things exist and that so-called things of the spirit, like love and courage, are illusions. This may be true, but can you prove it? What you really have done is to decide, as an act of will, to believe that it is so. You have deliberately chosen to narrow your understanding of the world so that it includes only "things." Materialism is your faith.

An adult convert accepts the Christian faith because he sees that Christianity makes more sense of life than any rival explanation. Christianity is the most probable hypothesis, the most adequate world-view. A frame which has room for both matter and spirit, for supernature as well as nature, enables us to see man and the world whole. With Christian premises a reasoned pattern can be discerned. The man with a world-view including only things and men, for example, will try to understand a friend's emotional disturbances simply as the result of a guilt complex. The Christian, whose world-view includes a moral universe, would be just as alert to the psychological realities but he has room in his diagnosis for the possibility that his friend actually is guilty. This diagnosis in turn would affect the proposed cure. Those with the narrower world-view can only suggest that he get rid of the idea of sin. Those with the broader Christian world-view can propose the resources of the forgiveness of sins.

But, broad or narrow, one's basic view of things is taken on faith.[1] Thus conversion to Christianity is always a change from one faith to another, not a change from no faith to faith. It may be a change from whatever the convert had previously thought to be ultimate. Going from one faith to another involves a leap, not to just any view but to the most plausible view.

Does one then ever know? Yes. A scientist does not waste chemicals testing every hypothesis which may come into his head. But he will test a plausible hypothesis, gambling some materials, counting the cost. If through repeated experiment the hypothesis makes coherent sense out of the data, and if reliable results ensue time after time, then he knows. So with the Christian hypothesis. It is tested in the laboratory of life. It is lived. This is the great gamble, the one for which Jesus asked us to count the cost. To make the test at all one must be willing to stake his life. When, now, better sense is made out of a man's life, when he is conscious of living in a fuller dimension, when he understands his past better, has a deeper inner peace in the midst of trials, and faces the future unafraid, in short, when he experiences our Lord's own promise, *I am come that they might have life and that they might have it more abundantly,* then he knows. Hypothesis is seen as truth.

FAITH IS PERSONAL

BECAUSE this is the nature of faith, we say at the beginning of the Creed, I believe *in,* not I believe *that. I believe in God*—Father, Son, and Holy Spirit. I put my trust in Him.

---

[1] Strictly speaking, it is only in this realm of ultimate conviction that we are dealing with faith. Faith in particular things or principles is really presupposition or hypothesis. There is a genuine analogy between the two, and hence for greater simplicity we have been using here the words interchangeably.

This is quite a different thing from saying, I believe that there is a God. That is an abstract conclusion of thought. Faith is the response of a person to a Person. This is the way with persons. When a man says he believes in his wife, he does not mean that he believes that she exists or that he has a wife. He means rather that he trusts her and that he has given himself to her for life.

In the Christian view of things, this response of person to Person is exactly what God wants. It is in the hope of it that God has made us. He does not primarily want our minds. Nor does He primarily want our deeds. He wants us. He has so made us that we shall never really be satisfied until we give ourselves to Him. St. Augustine wrote, "Thou hast made us for thyself and our hearts are restless until they rest in thee." Or, in the words of Julian Huxley, "The modern man has a God-shaped blank in his consciousness."

It must not be supposed, however, that man's search for God is like a one-way street in which the traffic is all toward God. True, men do search for God, and sometimes even before they know what they are seeking. But the Christian faith also proclaims that God is always searching for men. He seeks to reveal Himself to them in the glory of created things, through the lives of fellowmen, through the Holy Scriptures, through the fellowship of the Church, and through the inner stirrings of each man's heart. This is something the true convert always knows in his experience of faith. When once he has responded he knows it was in answer to a call. He knows that God was there first, seeking.

With some men this recognition is focused in an arresting dramatic event. St. Paul on the Damascus Road is the classic example. Quite different but equally crucial was

St. Augustine's experience. After years of intellectual inquiry and moral struggle, his actual decision for Christ was brought about by a quite simple event. Sitting in a garden he heard a child's voice coming from a house nearby, "Take up and read." He picked up his Bible, turned to *Romans,* and read, *Not in rioting and drunkenness, not in chambering and wantonness, not in strife and envying. But put ye on the Lord Jesus Christ.*

Different again, but equally definite, was John Wesley's experience. He thus recalls his conversion:

On May 24, 1738, I went very unwillingly to a society in Aldersgate Street, where one was reading Luther's preface to the *Epistle to the Romans.* About a quarter before nine, while he was thus describing the changes which God works in the heart through faith in Christ, I felt my heart strangely warmed; I felt I did trust in Christ, Christ alone, for salvation; and an assurance was given me that He had taken away my sins, even mine, and saved me from the law of sin and death.

With some men the conviction comes as it would in other significant concerns; truth compels the mind, and the will responds. Often the agent of such a conversion is a convincing book or a persuasive apologist, coming just as one is ready. This is the way it was with the Ethiopian eunuch whose story is told in *Acts 8.* A devout man, whose search for the true God had led him to Jerusalem to worship, he was pondering the meaning of the Suffering Servant passages in *Isaiah.* Philip, inspired to join him on his return home, interpreted the lines and explained their fulfillment in Jesus Christ, whom he preached to him. The Ethiopian was convinced, and when they next came to water, he said: *See, here is water; what doth hinder me to be baptized?*

With many another, conversion is the gradual growth in spiritual awareness, where God and His Kingdom move closer and closer to the center of a man's life. And even in a Paul or an Augustine or a Wesley, the moment of conversion was not really out of the blue. Looking back, the convert can see how all his life has converged toward this great inner event. He can see the part played by a chance meeting, by a certain book, by an all-consuming secular interest playing itself out, by a reaching up for help in moments of despair, by wistful yearnings mixed with the boredom of success, by the painful lesson of a failure.

There is great variety in the pattern of conversion because conversion is a personal experience, the confrontation of a person by a Person. However, we are confronted and whatever may be the manner and timing of our response, the One with whom we have to do is the same. It is He of whom we say, *I believe in one God.*

One God the Father Almighty, Maker of Heaven and Earth

AT THE center of all things is God. This conviction is basic in Christianity. Its creed is built around God and what God has done. It sees man and the world in their relationship to God, and insists that only in this fashion can either men or the world be rightly understood. The first volume in this series, *The Holy Scriptures* by Robert C. Dentan, made clear the fact that the Bible is concerned with God's mighty acts in history for man's redemption. The second volume, *Chapters in Church History* by P. M. Dawley, showed that the story of the Christian Church can be grasped only when it is seen as the continuing work of God in the history of men. We must attempt now to understand the Church's central theology, its affirmation about God.

The theology of the Christian faith is supremely important, not primarily because it is a good theory but because it is the ground and base for Christian living. It speaks with meaning to each of us because it tells him truths about himself, about his human situation, about the significance of life itself. To men who are confused and despairing, the Christian faith in God, the Father Almighty, Maker of heaven and earth, brings the only meaning that can endure, despite the changes and chances of our human lot. When we have wrestled with these Christian assertions about God, we shall see that they are necessary because they draw out the truth that is implicit in the experience of the believing man. They are involved in the life of the Christian Church. They are the foundation truths with which every man or woman is vitally concerned. For Christian faith in God is not a speculative matter. It is a faith for living.

GOD IS ULTIMATE

WHEN the Christian Church speaks of God, it means that He is the most important Reality of all realities. This is the very least which can be said about God. He is ultimate, final. The equation suggested by the late Archbishop Temple is altogether right, "God minus the world would still equal God; the world minus God would equal nothing." No Christian thinker has ever been satisfied with a view of God which suggested that He could be regarded as one among many. The entire scriptural witness rejects any such idea as blasphemous. Christian faith and experience testify that God is "that than which no greater can be conceived." We can think of no reality "more ultimate" than God. It is this particular theological assertion which makes the rest of Christian belief possible. If God is not the most important reality in life, then the remaining doctrines of the Christian faith are not worth bothering about.

35

Another way of putting this primary Christian belief is that God is the explanation or reason for all else that exists. Men wonder why there should be a world; God is the explanation. He is the Cause behind all lesser causes. Things do not explain themselves. There must be a final answer to the question, Why? That answer is what we mean by God.

The Bible's teaching about God is basic to Christianity. Its first stress is on the reality of God as supreme and final.

Before the mountains were brought forth, or ever the earth and the world were made, thou art God from everlasting, and world without end. (Psalm 90:2.)

Or, in the magnificent words of Psalm 102:25-27:

Thou, Lord, in the beginning hast laid the foundation of the earth, and the heavens are the work of thy hands.

They shall perish, but thou shalt endure; they all shall wax old as doth a garment;

And as a vesture shalt thou change them, and they shall be changed; but thou art the same, and thy years shall not fail.

It is with this God that men have to do. It is by Him that we are sought and confronted. As He is the ultimate and final One; He also is eternal. This was suggested in the phrases quoted from the Psalms; God is *from everlasting,* and *world without end.* The created world in which we live and of which we are a part does not endure. Nothing continues long in one stay. "Time like an ever-moving stream bears all its sons away." But God abides forever. That is why He is dependable. Before this world came into existence, God was. When it shall have passed away, God will still be. He *is;* the present tense of the verb must always be used when we are talking about Him.

GOD IS HOLY

Now the God who eternally is, is the altogether holy God. Holiness means more than that God is good. It means that God in the mystery of His being is so pure, so much Himself, that He can never be fathomed by the mind of man. He remains Himself, wonderful in His glory and majesty. *He is of purer eyes than to behold iniquity.* He is to be approached with awe, with reverence, with godly fear. The Bible speaks repeatedly of God's majestic selfhood, His transcendent grandeur, His mysterious glory. It is no wonder then that we feel our unworthiness before Him. When we draw nigh unto Him we must first seek to cleanse ourselves.

GOD IS LIVING

Furthermore, the God in whom Christians believe is a living God. Some people think of deity as an impersonal reality, static and inert. Some describe God as a great force or power. But Christians say that He is alive, dynamically alive, with an intensity of existence far above any that we can conceive. Moreover, He is alive as a personal being, who wills to be in relationship with His creation, who has a purpose in the world, who makes Himself known to His creatures and everlastingly works within them. The Bible is the record of the way in which God has done these things. It is not the complete record, of course, but it is the distinctive revelation of God's purpose and work. The Hebrew prophets discerned His hand in their own history and in the history of the other nations of the earth. The men and women of whose lives the Bible tells us are aware of God's presence and power. They never think of Him as aloof, remote, cold, impersonal. Rather, He is that One who is alive, He is the living God with whom all must reckon. He will not let men alone. He troubles them when they forget Him and He strengthens them when they seek Him.

In the very chapter (40) of Isaiah which gives the most exalted picture of God, who *sitteth upon the circle of the earth,* who *stretcheth out the heavens as a curtain,* the Prophet says that this same God *giveth power to the faint; and to them that have no might he increaseth strength.* God is not merely the ultimate and eternal Reality; He is also the personal God who comes to men to bind them to Himself and empower them with His own strength.

GOD HAS A PURPOSE

HE does these things with a purpose. He works through the world of nature and through history, so that *the heavens declare the glory of God;* the rise and fall of nations is in His hand: *The Lord liveth, which brought up and which led the seed of the house of Israel out of the north country, and from all countries whither I had driven them* (*Jeremiah 23:8*). What is more, He has dealings with men on personal terms: *The Lord is nigh unto all them that call upon him, to all that call upon him in truth* (*Psalm 145:18*).

GOD IS RIGHTEOUS

GOD is a righteous God. His purpose is to establish His justice in the earth. He seeks for righteousness among men. He brings the wicked to destruction. He desires goodness among His creatures, because He Himself is altogether good. He is indefatigable in His working and His purpose will be realized. Despite the evil imagination of men's hearts, His will shall be done. Each of these statements could be supported by extensive quotations from the Old Testament.[1] It must suffice to say that this is the heart of the biblical understanding of God; He is ultimate, eternal, purposive, personal, righteous, and unfailing. His plan cannot suffer defeat.

THE DEVELOPED CHRISTIAN TEACHING ABOUT GOD

AGAINST this biblical background, let us now set forth in more schematic style, the teaching about God which the Christian Church professes and upon which the Christian life is based.

Here we cannot avoid the theological language which has been developed by Christian thinking through the centuries. Every science has its own terms and Christian theology is no exception. The ideas which these terms express are not necessarily obscure. Indeed they are not at all so. But they demand the same kind of careful attention and precise thinking that might be expected of the painstaking statement of any truth. Nor are such statements theoretical or abstract; they all spring out of facts known in human experience. For the idea that God exists, and that we can know Him, did not first appear in the minds of speculative thinkers. It came out of the lives of men and women as they tried to make sense of what happened to them in their deepest moments. The most primitive people are aware of something outside themselves which awakens in them feelings of awe and reverence. That is why they worship. Even if their worship is directed through strange objects which seem superstitious to us, yet they are responding to something which is greater than themselves.,

---

[1] See *The Holy Scriptures* for an account of these and the other elements in the Biblical view of God.

Again, men everywhere sense the worth of high values like goodness and truth, and seek to understand their significance and their relation to the whole meaning of life. Finally, as we have indicated already, man's demand for some explanation of himself and his world has led him to the assertion that there is a First Cause and Final Explanation. It is from these concrete experiences of men that theology, in part, gets its data.

But there is something else which is of supreme importance: revelation. We shall devote considerable space to this in the latter part of this chapter. Here we point out that men in every part of the world, in all ages, have been certain that God has disclosed Himself to them unmistakably. Indeed the very experience of life itself implies this. For man is largely a responsive being, seeking to understand and to make meaning out of the rich and varied pressure of his world upon him. As that world moves in upon his tiny mind, he moves out to meet it. He responds. When he comes to think about this, he begins to see that the true meaning of things is being told to him, is being expressed, in all this. The truth of things is revealed to him. It is not revealed all at once, not all in the same way, not all with equal value and importance, but it *is* revealed. The story of man's religious life, from the earliest days down to the birth of the Christian faith, is the account of man's growing recognition that God's life is touching his life. The Holy Scriptures are both the record of the revelation God made to the Jewish people and to those who knew Jesus Christ, and the witness and response to that revelation.

Wherever and however the revelation takes place, man responds to this movement of God toward him. Man experiences that which demands worship because it is holy. He ascribes worth to goodness and beauty, truth and righteousness. He senses that there is an ultimate explanation and all-including Reality with which, or with whom, he must make terms. In all these ways, man comes to see God as possessing the characteristics by which He is described in Christian theology.

But Supernatural Reality is above and beyond that which man can completely define and describe. Hence our assertions about God's nature are made with certitude, but also with profound humility. Nor are these assertions merely an exercise of human reason. Every one of the attributes has its place in the portrait of God's nature which is given to us in the Holy Scriptures, by whose witness all have been tested and proved in the course of the Church's life.

THE ESSENTIAL ATTRIBUTES

THE Church's theology has consistently spoken of the attributes of God; His characteristics. These attributes are of two kinds: metaphysical and qualitative. The metaphysical attributes are given to us in the very notion of God itself. Some of them have been called essential, dealing with God as He is in Himself; others are relative or concerned with God's relation to His world. Those which are qualitative have to do with the character of God: what sort of a God He is, what He is like.

God, then, is the ultimate and eternal Reality who forever seeks and confronts man. Certain things may be seen at once to be true of God. In the first place He exists of Himself. He depends upon nothing but Himself. That is, He is self-existent. The world which God has created is the freely willed result of His purpose. God does not depend upon it in any sense whatsoever. Theologians have a word for this, *aseity* (from-himself-ness). It is the basic attribute of Deity. If God is not a being like this, He is not really in control of things. If He is not like this, there may be reaches of the universe which are beyond His sovereign rule. But such a thought is a contradiction both of religious conviction and of sound reason. For man in his encounter with God is certain that God is the only being who explains Himself and requires nothing else to explain Him. It is clear that if there be anything which is genuinely ultimate, it must be independent and self-existent. How could the ultimate receive its meaning from that which is not ultimate? It would be a contradiction in terms. The Prophet Isaiah declared this, *I am the Lord, and there is none else, there is no God beside me (Isaiah 45:5).*

Furthermore, God is infinite, far beyond the limitations of our human littleness. Infinite, of course, does not mean that God is very big. It means that size is irrelevant to Him. He cannot be measured quantitatively. When we claim that God is like this, we also are safeguarding the great religious conviction that the tiniest things in creation, as well as the biggest, are important to God. Again, our experience of finite things, the things with which we live and which we see and know in day-by-day living, is that they come and go, they are large or small, they grow or decrease, they change. They are dependent on other things. But God is not like this. As Psalm 102 records: *My days are gone like a shadow, and I am withered like grass. But thou, O Lord, shalt endure for ever, and thy remembrance throughout all generations.*

Because He is infinite, He is also inscrutable. He cannot be fully comprehended or grasped by the mind of man. After all, our human intelligence is fitted for a sort of piecemeal learning about the things which we see and touch and taste and hear. It is not made to grasp, in any full and final sense, the infinite and ultimate. If we had to depend upon our minds alone, or were obliged to be content only with the evidence of our senses, we could never reach to God as Christians know Him. The fact of our human finitude makes this absolutely certain. If we can never entirely understand the spots on the back of a beetle, as one great philosopher pointed out, how could we ever hope to understand the reality of God? St. Paul's great cry, found in his letter to the Romans (*11:33*) puts this truth, *O the depth of the riches both of the wisdom and knowledge of God! how unsearchable are his judgments, and his ways past finding out!* On the other hand, as we have seen, we can know something about God. Any attempt to make sense of experience leads us to recognize certain truths about the ultimate Reality. Much more important than this, however, is the Christian conviction that we can know something about God because God has actually disclosed Himself to us. This is revelation. And Christians say, with the author of the Fourth Gospel, that while *no man hath seen God at any time, the only begotten Son, who is in the bosom of the Father, he hath declared him* (*St. John 1:18*).

Again, God is a unity. If there is any explanation of the world in which we live, it is the *one* explanation. If there is any ultimate, it must be the ultimate. To say anything else would be a contradiction in terms. There is a oneness, an all-of-a-piece quality, about God. Here the scriptural record is of enormous importance. For Judaism taught that there is one God, that He is unique, *Hear, O Israel, the Lord thy God is one Lord (Deuteronomy 6:4)*. In Him purpose and character and nature form a single unity, whose quality is Holy Love.

We do not speak of *it* when we talk of God. We speak of *Him*. That means that God is better understood as being personal than as being impersonal. Obviously He is not a person in just the same sense in which you and I are persons. That would be quite absurd, for it would deny the infinite nature of God and His inscrutable quality. Everyone knows that it is impossible completely to understand another human personality. God's personality is far above that of any man, hence it is mysterious to us. But at the same time, it is wrong to think of God as not being personal at all. For if we should say this, we should be saying that the creation which God has made possesses intelligence, freedom, purpose, the capacity to communicate itself, while the God who made it is lacking all these. That certainly would be nonsense. When we ascribe personality to God, therefore, we are saying that in some wonderful way, far beyond our human imagining, God is One who knows both Himself and His world. He is free in His nature and not bound by chains of imposed necessity. He has a purpose which He wills to carry out. He can and does enter into communion with that which is not Himself. He is not like sticks and stones, unconscious forces or energies, half-personalized beings like animals. He is like, although not just like, a human person. It is hardly necessary to point out the obvious fact that the whole of the scriptural record, as well as all Christian experience, testifies to the personal relationship which men have with the God who is Himself personal.

44

Finally, as already has been implied, God is One to whom all time and all space are a present experience. He is a spiritual being, without a physical body. Therefore, He is not bound down by the limitations in time and space which beset us. As the theologians say, He is both immensurable (beyond measurement by yardsticks) and eternal (beyond measurement by clocks or calendars). These assertions are plainly implied if God is indeed infinite. That word means not limited, and a God who could be measured or timed would be less than the ultimate Reality in whom Christian faith is placed.

THE RELATIVE ATTRIBUTES

THE last two attributes, although often classed as essential, lead us directly into what are called the relative or active attributes. For they describe the way in which God is related to the world which He has made. God is active toward His creation. He works in it and through it, He is carrying out a plan or purpose. To do that, it is plain, God must possess the power to perform that which He wills. The word used to describe this is omnipotence.

Few words have been so misunderstood as this one. It does not mean that God can do anything whatsoever. For example, if God be the Truth about things, He cannot do things that are self-contradictory. He cannot make squares which are circles. He cannot make black which is white. He cannot make good which is bad. Above all, He cannot do that which is contrary to His own nature. On the other hand, all the power there is, wherever it is, comes from Him, as Creator. Of course that power can be used against Him. A small child can take his father's gift and use it in ways that are against the father's will or desire. So men can take the power God gives them, and because of their freedom, pervert it to their own selfish ends. This in fact is precisely what man does over and over again. But it is still God's power which is being used. That is why man's misuse of his freedom is sinful.

But God's power is manifested in still another way. His omnipotence is such that He can make even man's wrath turn to His praise (*Psalm 76:10*). He grants men freedom; but at the same time He uses that freedom of man's to carry out, in the long run, the divine plan. He can never be defeated.

God is also omnipresent. St. Thomas Aquinas said that God's omnipresence means that everything, everywhere, is always present to God. He is as much in one place as in another, although He may and does will to make Himself known more fully here or there. His energizing power is everywhere at work, in every range and level of creation. Yet He wills to act more intensely and directly at certain times or places than elsewhere. Even while He is omnipresent, He is free to do this or that, according to His plan for His creation.

In the now of God's life, all the successive events and places and times of our world's history are known and understood. That implies that God is not only omnipresent. He is also omniscient. Past, present, future are open to His knowledge. To God *all hearts are open, all desires known*. From Him *no secrets are hid*. Yet this should not suggest that His creatures are deprived of genuine freedom. A father knows his son's mind and may even know what he will do, but he does not by this fact destroy the freedom of his child.

But this means that the divine wisdom is something much greater than our human knowledge. It includes everything that has been, that is, or that can be; and it includes these within one great all-encompassing will. For God is working out His purpose not only in the light of the over-all plan which He has for His creation, but also in the light of the day-by-day happenings which take place in that creation. What kind of a God, then, is this God in whom we believe? What is His character?

THE QUALITATIVE OR MORAL ATTRIBUTES

To ask such questions is to ask what are the qualitative or moral attributes of God. Here, as elsewhere, when we think about God we must use our reason and reflect upon our experience. We must consider the facts of our human life and experience and see what they may teach us about our Creator. There is no way by which we can escape this kind of limited anthropomorphism.[2] We have to think of the ultimate Reality in terms of our human life. If we try to avoid thinking of God in this fashion, we shall think of Him as though He were either a machine or a blind force. Personality as we experience it is the most valuable thing we know. It is therefore the most valuable clue we have to the nature of God.

Thus men have said that God is good. He has a nature of overflowing, superabundant goodness. He cares for all His works. God is just. He gives to each that which is its due. He is merciful; He gives more than we deserve, more even than we desire. He is blessed. In His inner life, He is utter, unspeakably rich joy. Above all, and here we are presuming to say more than man, it might be thought, would dare, He is loving. At the very heart of things, there is burning, consuming, all-embracing Love. This is what

---

[2] This means that we think about God in human terms.

we mean when we call God our Father. He is concerned for us, He cares for every one of us. But He is not a sentimental Father. Rather He is one who loves us so much that He will spare neither Himself nor us, to the end that we may really become His children and find supreme happiness in doing His holy will.

REVELATION

To say such things about God is to make assertions which are almost impudent in their audacity. The mind of man can hardly conceive such thoughts about God. How dare we say that God is Love? So as we have already shown earlier, the necessity for the idea of revelation is evident to us. That which the mind of man could only faintly glimpse and the tongue of man assert hesitantly and wistfully, the Christian can declare with bold confidence. He can do this for one reason only. God who is ultimate, eternal, one; God who has a purpose and plan; God who desires to be known by men, is also the God who reveals Himself. Out of the mystery by which our humanity is surrounded, comes the voice of God, speaking to us men. The Word of God, that is the revelation or self-expression of God, comes to us and speaks to us by the prophets. But in Jesus Christ He takes on the flesh and blood, mind and soul, of our humanity. That is why we can venture to say these things about the kind of God He is.

For the whole of Christian teaching about God rests not so much upon what human reason can give, although it takes serious account of these truths, as it does upon what God has revealed Himself to be. In the holiness of God, the mystery of His selfhood which we cannot enter nor understand, there is a heart of love which seeks to

find men and to bring them into close and loving relationship with their eternal Father. Just as one of us, wish-
ing to enter into friendship with another, will move out
toward him and seek to open up a channel of communication with him, so it is with God. God reveals Himself,
He tells us about Himself.

GOD THE LIVING CREATOR

BUT God's language, in revelation, is not the language of
nouns and adjectives. It is the language of verbs, that is,
action. God's way is not to drop messages about Himself
from heaven. God does things. The Jewish people knew
Him as the living God. A living being is one who is active,
whose actions make him known to others, whose actions
express the innermost quality of his life and nature. God
acts in nature and in history, so that He may be known
and loved.

The whole of the creation is an act of God. For the
meaning of creation itself is that it depends upon God,
who upholds it in being and keeps it as His own. Creation
does not mean that God once upon a time made the world
and then left it alone. On the contrary, creation means
that at every moment, from the beginning of time, God's
action continually sustains the world. As Alfred Noyes
has written: "Now, and forever, God makes earth and
heaven." Creation is God's action in bringing into existence that which is not Himself, in keeping it in being, in
working through it and in it so that great purposes may
be accomplished. The fact of God's creative activity is
seen throughout the universe. He is creatively active in
the world of electrons and atoms and molecules and in
all forms of creation up to the highest things that have

49

emerged, such as man with his knowledge of goodness and truth and beauty. God is the God of the entire world; it is all His handiwork, evil alone excepted.

It makes no difference to the Christian faith whether God created the world at the beginning instantaneously, or whether the creation was a long process and is perhaps even now incomplete. Scientists tell us that the process seems to be a slow one. And the Anglican Communion finds no conflict on this point between Christian faith and the conclusions of science. As a matter of fact, the newer scientific insights make it possible for us to have a greater idea of the divine creativity. God is always in the beginning, before anything comes to be. He is the reason for its coming to be. He is the inexhaustible Source from which it all comes. The very richness and variety of the world which scientific study has disclosed makes it possible for us to grasp something of the inexpressible wealth of God Himself. If God's creation is so wonderful, how much more wonderful must God be! But in any event, evolution is a scientific concept which in no way negates the religious truth that God is the Creator, the ultimate meaning of all things.

Yet God acts more intimately and directly in history than He does in nature. This is what we might expect, if God is personal. For in men, with their capacity to act freely and with their minds open to knowledge, there is the possibility of a movement of God which is not found in the inanimate and unconscious orders of creation. God enters, through His Spirit, into the souls of the prophets and seers. He inspires them to see His hand in all His works. The nations of the earth are held in the hollow of His hand. He brings mighty things to pass among them. The Old Testament is one long witness to this fact. God's

outgoing, creative, self-expressive nature, which we call
His Word, is both the ground of all creation and the
moving force through all history. Above all, that Word
is at work in the affairs of men. The Word of God who
became flesh and dwelt among us in Jesus our Lord and
Saviour, is the self-same Word by whom all things were
made. The Word is the light of men, coming to His own
even when they will not receive Him.[3]

REVELATION AND THE KNOWLEDGE OF GOD

Now we come full circle. For it is because of God's expressive action or revelation and because of our thoughts
about the richness of His action, that we have been able
to give any description of God at all. Of course such description is never perfect. As St. Paul says (*I Corinthians
13:12*) *we see through a glass, darkly.* But since God has
revealed Himself, we know with a certainty that He is, that
He is good, that He has a purpose for us, that He is altogether to be trusted. We know that if we live in Him and
for Him we can commit our lives to His keeping for time
and for eternity. By ourselves, apart from revelation, we
could never have said these things. Thanks to God's
gracious self-disclosure, we can affirm them with complete
confidence.

Such a confidence is intimately related to the providence of God. If God has a plan for His world and if each
person and every thing in the world fits into that plan,
then we can be sure that *the very hairs of your head are all
numbered* (*St. Matthew 10:30*). When Jesus gave us this
assurance, He was making it clear that whatever men need
in their life with Him, God will provide. This is what the

---

[3] The last two sentences are a paraphrase of the opening verses of St.
John's Gospel.

Christian doctrine of providence means. It does not mean that "all things work together for good." This is an inaccurate translation of St. Paul's words. What he said was, *God works all things together for good with them that love him (Romans 8:28 RSV).* When we are in fellowship with the God who reveals Himself to man and are seeking to do His will in our lives, we can be sure that He will provide for us. This does not mean that we shall be spared difficulties, problems, the need for planning, the pains of human life. After all, God did not spare His Son, Jesus Christ, the pain of the Cross. Yet everything that comes in our path, like the Cross itself, can be made a way to the fulfillment of God's will. God's grace is sufficient to do these things.

GOOD AND EVIL

BUT what about the evil in the world? It is very real and it must be faced. The Christian who has faith in God does not shut his eyes to the fact of evil. God is good and there is evil. We can never hope for a full explanation of these apparently contradictory truths. Because our minds are finite, we cannot grasp the complete truth about matters like this. We can indeed do something to explain the suffering and the evil that come from man's sin. After all, this is a necessary possibility of the freedom which God has given us. Freedom is freedom to do evil as well as to do good.

But beyond this the best way of talking about evil is to say something like this: The world is still in the making, like a shop in which something is being created with the edges not yet smoothed, the full design not yet plainly seen. In that world, some of what we call evil seem to be part of the necessary structure—such things as tidal waves and earthquakes. Some come from our close human solidarity, so that we suffer in and with our brethren in the world. Some are due to human ignorance or stupidity. Much we cannot explain at all. But Christianity has no theoretical or speculative solution of evil, pain, suffering, although it offers many hints looking toward an answer. It has, however, a practical working-solution.

That solution, which comes to us not by human thinking but by divine revelation, is centered in the Cross of Jesus Christ. We come now very near to the topics which will be discussed in succeeding chapters. But this much must be said now: if the central Christian faith, that God was in Christ reconciling the world to Himself, be true, then we know that God is with us in our experience of pain and suffering and evil. In the unique human life which He created for Himself and united with Himself, in Jesus Christ our Lord, He knows what it is to face evil and pain, to meet defeat and death. Because He has done these things and faced the worst that man can know, we have the certainty that even in the valley of the shadow of death God is with us and we need have no fear. Christian faith and hope, strong and courageous, look at the Cross and affirm, *we are more than conquerors through him that loved us (Romans 8:37).*

THEOLOGY AS THE BASIS FOR CHRISTIAN LIFE

EVERY theological assertion made in this chapter has its direct bearing upon the day-by-day life of the Christian believer. The fact, for example, that God is creator of the world means that each one of us is a living creature, because we depend upon God for all that we are and have, *for our creation, preservation, and all the blessings of this life.* This implies that the sense of our creatureliness, our being utterly dependent upon Him who made us, and not upon ourselves, is a characteristic of those who know the truth about their own existence. Again, the teaching about providence makes it clear that we are rooted in God and that, if we trust in Him, we can live meaningful lives under His governance. To take a third example, the assertion of God's omnipotence enables us to live as those safe from every danger and furnished with every requirement, since God is ultimately in control of His creation. Hence the heart which is guarded and strengthened by God can be fearless and at peace, no matter how perilous the times may be. These are but three illustrations of what is currently called the existential quality of Christian faith. Our faith has a vital and personal meaning which speaks directly to every man, as well as to the society of which he is a part.

Christianity is a faith which can be lived, for it is faith in the living God who judges us and loves us. It is not a speculation. It has been forged in the furnace of human experience, as men and women have found themselves confronted by the reality of God who made them. Above all the faith has been forged by those who, in Christ and through His Spirit in the Church, have been redeemed from sin and have received power which gives their life meaning and makes it rich and full in Him.

Theology, then, is important because it safeguards perennial truths derived from the facts of the divine-human encounter. The Christian affirmations about God are the very life-stuff of the whole Christian way. They are central, because God Himself is the center of life. Without Him, nothing has sense or significance. By faith in Him and communion with Him we are enabled truly to live.

54

For Us Men

IN the seventh century, when Christianity was brought to Anglo-Saxon England, a missionary named Paulinus made his way to the court of the powerful King Edwin of Northumbria. There he was treated with polite-ness and permitted to make converts, although the king himself remained well disposed but unconvinced. At last, in 627, increasingly drawn toward baptism, Edwin called his counselors together and asked their opinion of the new faith. The reply of one old earl has become famous from the account given by the Venerable Bede in his *Ecclesiastical History:*

O King, this present life of man, compared with that time which is beyond, which is unknown to us, seems to me like this: When you are sitting with your aldermen and nobles at supper in wintertime, with a bright fire burning in the midst of the hall, while outside the rain and snow are beating against the walls—lo! a sparrow flies swiftly in at one door, and swiftly through the hall, and out at an-other. He was safe for a moment from the wintry storm while he was indoors, but after that short spell of warmth he disappears. From winter he came in and to winter he goes out. Such is the life of man: he appears for a little while. But what went before? And what will follow after? This we do not know. Therefore if this new teaching bring us anything more sure it is worth our following.

The human situation has not changed since 627. Man is a problem to himself, and Christianity meets this problem with an answer.

The first Office of Instruction begins with the individual. *What is your Christian Name?* This question goes right to the heart of the matter. You are a human being who bears a Christian name. The Christian name, at once recalling your baptism, points to a place for you in a scheme that encompasses the old earl's question *From what?* and *To what?* The Christian understanding of life holds an answer to these questions. It has an interpretation of man. There are other interpretations also, but none which looks with such unsparing realism at all the facts of human experience and makes sense of them.

HOW MAN DIFFERS FROM OTHER ANIMALS

THERE is general agreement now that man is a latecomer in the world. The writer of *Genesis* used great insight in assigning the creation of man to the sixth and last day of creation. Man did not make the natural world. He was not on hand to witness its ages of growth. Human history comes as a late chapter in natural history. If we care to study only the properties that man has in common with the oyster, the question *Whence?* could receive the answer, From ancestral organisms; and the question *Whither?* could receive the answer, To an earthly or a watery grave.

But man shows characteristics which make him different

from all other organisms. Chemically and biologically it is at times convenient to treat man as an animal. Nevertheless, he is an animal with a difference.

Familiar peculiarities set man apart from the lower animals. Man's 'physical characteristics are significant. The structure of man's hands, for example, is extremely flexible, especially because the thumb faces the fingers, and his hands and arms are equally adaptable to heavy work and to delicate manipulation. Yet at birth his physical capacities (in comparison, for instance, with a colt or calf) are quite undeveloped. It takes a human body months, instead of minutes or hours, merely to learn to walk; and it takes years to attain maturity. For this reason a child is dependent for a long time upon his parents. In large measure what he is and will become depends upon their attitudes, their relations to each other and to him.

And throughout life a man needs a supporting society. Learning largely takes the place of instinct. Each man must be educated. The old set the examples for the young and hand down traditions and values to them, and this is part of a continuous process called culture. Wherever men dwell, they live in organized societies.

Man has distinctive capacities and interests. With his agile hands he makes tools and machines that greatly increase his productivity. He thinks of himself as a molder, maker, manipulator. He develops writing, arts, and crafts. With his mental gifts he remembers and foresees. He develops the power of reflective thinking, abstraction, comparison, and symbolizing. He generalizes. He speaks, and the speech of even the most uncivilized tribes is not as we often imagine, a series of brutal grunts, but constitutes, in each case, a language in the full sense, complete with

57

grammar and inflections. He recognizes obligation. He knows what it is to initiate, to feel responsible, to feel guilty, and to be discontented. He has a sense of humor, and is able to laugh even at himself. In all these ways man is more than an animal.

But the being that has all these endowments, man, is comparatively small and weak. He could scarcely exist at all without his hard-earned cultural lore and his practical ingenuity. Man is not as big as an elephant, nor as strong as a mule, nor as swift as a gazelle, nor as at home in the water as a fish; and for him as for them, death is inescapable. He will die; but, unlike the beasts, he knows that he is going to do so. He is subject to diseases and disasters in great variety. And because he is intelligent and foresighted he knows this weakness.

MAN'S LIMITATIONS AND DIFFICULTIES

ABLE to form and appreciate general ideas, a man is capable of perceiving what a very small item in the universe he is. Able to plan, he is the constant victim of disappointments. He is capable of knowledge, and, knowing, is acutely conscious of his ignorance. His boundless imagination makes all limitation irksome. As Shakespeare writes in *Hamlet:* "What a piece of work is man. How noble in reason! How infinite in faculty! In form and moving how express and admirable! In action how like an angel! In apprehension how like a god!"

But a clearer reflection of man's true situation can be found in some words of St. Augustine, written a millenium and a half ago in his *City of God:*

That the whole human race has been condemned in its first origin, this life itself, if life it is to be called, bears witness by the hosts of cruel ills with which it is filled . . . What numberless extremes threaten our bodies from without—heat and cold, storms, floods, inundations, lightning, thunder, hail, earthquakes, houses falling, the stumbling and shying of horses, countless poisons in fruits, water, air, animals . . . What man can go out of his own house without being exposed on all hands to unforeseen accidents? Returning home sound in limb, he slips on his own doorstep, breaks his leg and never recovers.

Of course, in our part of the earth we have learned how to control a few of the more annoying physical ills, to take precaution against pain, and to reduce the chances of some kinds of accidents. But even if the span of life is a little longer in societies that are wealthy enough to afford the luxuries of medicine and sanitation, it nevertheless remains always precarious and painful. There is a threshold for every individual beyond which mental and physical suffering cannot be escaped, nor death avoided.

Man's social nature intensifies his problem. The things that cause us greatest grief are the things we do to one another. To the catalog of cruel ills already mentioned, St. Augustine goes on to add such things as quarrels, lawsuits, wars, and treason; anger, hatred, falsehood, robbery; murder, tyranny, cruelty, and luxury. And if education is the remedy, then, he suggests, it is a remedy nearly as painful as the disease. "What mean pedagogues, masters, the birch, the strap, the cane?" Added to the obstinacy of parents (who "rarely wish anything useful to be taught") the troubles of teaching and learning go deep into the contradiction of man himself.

Try as we will, we remember with difficulty and without difficulty forget. We learn with difficulty and without difficulty remain ignorant. We are diligent with difficulty and without difficulty are indolent.

Of course, one may well ask: Has there been no progress over the centuries? Are we not better off now than in the those troubled days of the fifth century? Certainly there has been a great increase in human knowledge, and education has become in some respects a little more painless. But this increase in knowledge has not even begun to eliminate the evil in the world. On the contrary, it has often armed it with new weapons. The plunderings, quarrels, and wars that distressed St. Augustine seem mild indeed in comparison with a full-scale modern war. The atrocities of the Nazis at the Buchenwald concentration camp were planned and carried out by people with college degrees and professional training. The evidence is stronger now than in any other age that our most disturbing difficulties do not lie in the realm of knowledge and technics, but in the realm of will and purpose. The difficulty is inside us.

Man's great accomplishments as philosopher, scientist, artist, and engineer neither assure his happiness nor protect him from certain compelling impulses which cause him to overreach and destroy. Our creative and our destructive powers take their rise from a quality of life that is profoundly human. No single word describes this quality, but it might be called a homelessness, a restlessness, or a chronic discontent. The capacity that we have to describe our own dilemmas has a good deal to do with it. We look at ourselves as if from the outside. We are self-conscious and self-critical. We judge ourselves and we deceive ourselves. We assign ourselves ideal rôles, and then fall short as we try to play them. Failure may render us abject. Just as frequently we try to find our way out by bluster, denial, hypocrisy, or violence.

Man, forever the hero and the villain in his own play, is never satisfied merely to carry out a rôle assigned by nature. He has the capacity to describe, to question, to foresee, to plan, and to change. He has the capacity of criticism, and he has the gift of dissatisfaction both with himself and with what is his. He has an endless discontent with every given state of things and an insecurity of spirit which drives him on to a hopeless quest for pleasure and an endless search for peace.

The suggestion, therefore, that what men need most is just to be natural begs all the questions. We know too much to accept ourselves and our world as final. In practice we can never treat the world as an order where we fit permanently and unquestioningly. Yet we find ourselves clinging to this or that illusory finality such as cash in the bank, a promising career, a degree of prestige, or the hope of a rest that never comes. And our experiences are always out of step with our hopes. History is strewn with declarations that this or that human achievement is final, certain, perfect, but nothing in ourselves nor in our world meets this expectation.

THE SOURCE OF MAN'S DISSATISFACTION

THE Christian religion has always been aware of the complexity of man's nature. It recognizes that the core of this elastic nature is his freedom. Man has a range of choices open to him, all entailing consequences. He has no fixed rôle in a neat order, but the rôle of a creator-and-destroyer within the limits of the created order. Man is the author of his own tragedy. His gift of freedom makes it possible

61

for him to create evil. And the conditions under which he has to exercise his gift makes it almost impossible that he should do otherwise.

Christianity recognizes man's restlessness. His will-o'-the-wisp chase of happiness and his diabolical attraction to extremes characterize a being who craves to possess and be possessed by something beyond himself which cannot be contained by him nor explained by him. Is it a comfortable home? Is it success in a career? Is it a happy marriage? Is it a statue in the park? Each of these offers its own kind of security against loneliness. But no one of them, nor all taken together (and how hard it is to make a harmony of them!), can satisfy the human seeker nor account for his dissatisfaction. *What does account for that dissatisfaction is man's need for God*. This is often the unconscious motivation for his extravagant actions.

Christianity understands the homelessness and wretchedness of the human spirit when it is separated from God. Thus, as the Bible makes clear, man's freedom and restlessness are not meaningless. They are indications of the destiny for man never to be fully realized in himself or his world. They show him drawn toward a purpose not of his own invention, as the child of God created in the image of God. The most perverse man desires God even without knowing what it is he wants. Men may pursue other ends but it is always God that draws them on. This is nowhere more strikingly expressed than in the passionate cry of Dmitri in Dostoevsky's *The Brothers Karamazov,* "Though I be following the devil, I am thy son, O Lord, and I love thee, and I feel the joy without which the world cannot stand."

The highest reach of man's freedom is to become aware

of this destiny and to offer himself fully and unreservedly to God. We are so made as to be free to love God or to reject Him. We are so constituted as to know and to enjoy that personal Being who seeks us out and who says to us in every creaturely situation, "I am more than all these." This is the cause of our restlessness in the presence of all created things. At one extreme, man's capacity to love carries him to such love of God that he forgets himself. At the other extreme stands his love of self or his selfish love of other creatures making him forget God. On our freedom to love God rests even our liberty of ordinary moral choice, because the real meaning of every choice between better and worse is choice of what draws us to God or draws us away from Him.

The use of our freedom in such a way as to reject God is called sin. Sin is the offering of one's self to something less than God. This means that our relationship to God is thereby broken. When we sin, we use our freedom for the purposes of self-assertion and self-will. The result of this is separation.

THE MISUSE OF FREEDOM: ORIGINAL SIN

THIS separation involves us in reducing or dismissing our consciousness of responsibility toward God, and in asserting ourselves as man against nature and man against man. When St. Augustine says that we find it easier to forget than to remember and easier to be ignorant than to learn, he is touching lightly on a puzzle that he himself clearly recognizes. It is that the thing that comes easiest to us is selfishness. Yet the suffering that always follows teaches us that we cannot imagine anything less likely to bring either peace or happiness. To say that we have a decided bent toward self-assertion is to say that we have a decided bent toward sin. Archbishop Temple writes in his *Christianity and Social Order:*

When we open our eyes as babies we see the world stretching out around us; we are in the middle of it; all proportions and perspectives in what we see are determined by the relation—distance, height, and so forth—of the various visible objects to ourselves. This will remain true of our bodily vision as long as we live. I am the center of the world I see; where the horizon is depends on where I stand. Now just the same thing is true at first of our mental and spiritual vision. Some things hurt us; we hope they will not happen again; we call them bad. Some things please us; we hope they will happen again; we call them good. Our standard of value is the way the things affect ourselves. So each of us takes his place in the center of his own world. But I am not the center of the world, or the standard of reference as between good and bad; I am not, and God is.

Since the sources of man's restlessness, his powers of appraisal, judgment, and criticism, are a divine gift, they are in some respects wholesome and creative. Without them he would not be only *a little lower than the angels;* he would not be man at all as we have been describing him. Since man's first use of these powers is, for whatever reason, in actual fact self-centered and without regard to God, we must expect to find disorder, strife, and suffering.

When freedom is used for reckless self-assertion (I *want what* I *want when* I *want it*) the result is a disordering of life. Putting myself, from the very beginning, in God's place means that (as Temple continues):

I am in a state, from birth, in which I shall bring disaster on myself and everyone affected by my conduct un-

64

less I can escape from it. Education may make my self-centeredness less disastrous by widening my horizon of interest; so far it is like the climbing of a tower which widens the horizon for physical vision while leaving me still the center and standard of reference. Education may do more than this if it succeeds in winning me into devotion to truth or to beauty; that devotion may effect a partial deliverance from self-centeredness. But complete deliverance can be effected only by the winning of my whole heart's devotion, the total allegiance of my will—and this only the Divine Love disclosed by Christ in His Life and Death can do.

Each assertion of ourselves, then, in such a way as to seek to exclude God damages the sinner. His own integrity is impaired when he lavishes his love on something less than the Greatest open to him. Each disordering of his own life in turn brings disorder into the lives of those around him. The sins of parents spread like an infection to their children. We witness the rise of sinful cultures, sinful institutions, sinful nations; the work, in short, of a sinful race of men. Very soon we find ourselves unable to understand our problems. With the best of intentions, so it seems to us, we succumb. We find ourselves exchanging freedom for slavery and then rebelling impotently at the result.

THE FALLEN STATE OF MAN

THE whole tragic situation which follows from sin and then in turn promotes sin, involving us all in its web, is called in Christian theology MAN'S FALLEN STATE. The tendency of man (which goes back as far as we can trace his history) to make self-assertion primary is called ORIGINAL SIN. Each of us is born with it. "From the beginning," says Temple in another part of the passage just quoted, "I put myself in God's place. This is my original sin. I was doing it before I could speak, and everyone else has been doing it from earliest infancy."

Furthermore, the terms *fallen state* and *original sin* remind us that the disaster toward which our life is pointed is social as well as individual. The disharmonies of life are not all accounted for by merely adding up individual sins. All human actions take place in a social structure that, so far as we know it, is from the beginning already warped by sin. It is partly true that we are sinners because we live in a sinful world. If there is an inhuman slum in my city, it may not be my fault as a private individual, but very likely its presence owes something to my sins of omission and commission as a citizen of my town, whose laws and practices permit its existence.

A PICTURE OF THE HUMAN PREDICAMENT

PERHAPS no Christian idea has been more misunderstood than this one of original sin. It has little to do with the question of where or when the first sin was committed. The story of Adam and Eve in *Genesis* is an illustrative story with man's primal sin and fall as its theme. It is not like a reporter's firsthand account. It is a dramatic picture, imaginative in detail and profound in its insight. It does not mean, as is popularly assumed, that every human being originates in sin because of the supposedly sinful nature of the sex relation. What it does mean is this. Man, being made free, is accountable for his own condition. There is a contrast between the truth that man is made with the capacity of freedom to know and love God, and the everyday fact that, left to himself, he does not ac-

66

tually use his freedom in this way. The contrast is of man's own making, the consequence of human will and not of God's will.

Why is man, though endowed with freedom, everywhere in chains? Why, if all men desire God, are they perpetually seeking and serving things infinitely less than God? The answer lies in the character of men's choices as a whole, and their use of their freedom. The situation as a whole is not the fault of this man or that, even though each is responsible for his own part in the general disorder. It is not the fault of the generation just past nor of the one before it. The fact is that every man in every age is born into a sinful world, into an environment already corrupted. This and not an inherent sinfulness in the sexual relation is the meaning of the familiar verse in Psalm 51, used in the Penitential Office, *Behold, I was shapen in wickedness, and in sin hath my mother conceived me.*

The universal condition reflects the way in which the freedom and happiness of any man involves, and is involved in, the freedom and happiness of every other. One single sin, committed anywhere, by anyone, opens the way to other sins, and like a crack in a dike invites the flood. Strictly speaking a man is guilty not because of original sin but because of his own actual sins. Yet, more profoundly, guilt reflects our alienation from God which comes primarily not from our single sins but from the self-centeredness and idol worship which are the roots of our sins. It is this that is the ground of man's universal sense of anxiety, which has close psychological ties to the equally widespread sense of guilt.

Now we can appreciate the biblical picture of what the first sin must have been like. The opening chapter of

Genesis recounts that on the last day of creation man was created and he was made in the image of God. He was endowed with certain God-like properties. He was to possess powers over and above those of his companions, the animals, for he was given *dominion over the fish of the sea, and over the fowl of the air, and over every living thing that moveth upon the earth* (*Genesis 1:28*). To every animal, also, he gave its name, a suggestion both of language and of the human faculty to generalize and classify. At once it was apparent that man must live in a society (*it is not good that the man should be alone*) and human society began with the beginning of the first family. Most momentous of all, it was given to man to choose his obedience to God. All the trees of the garden where he lived might be used as he liked, with one exception from which he was to abstain on penalty of death. Thereupon he made his fateful decision to disobey, an act of sheer self-assertion and contempt of God. (*Ye shall be as gods,* said the serpent to Eve.) Therefore he felt alienated also from God and hid at the sound of God's voice. Feeling guilty, he attempted to cover his nakedness. After vain efforts to evade responsibility and put the blame elsewhere he lost the garden and from that time forward, says *Genesis,* his daily work became a burden. It was decreed that henceforth birth was to be with suffering and death with ignominy.

But the story does not end here. Pride in the first generation led to murder in the second: Cain killed Abel. Crafts multiply; so do the evils of society. God intervenes to make a new start; the Flood leaves a remnant. But after a few generations the Fall was reënacted: men would build a tower to Heaven—a dramatic symbol, indeed, of man's "declaration of independence." But they cannot finish the

68

tower for they are unable to work together; they can no longer understand each other: Babel becomes babble. Men separate themselves from each other, the perennial consequence of separation from God.

This is the bare outline of the shrewd yet simple saga. Its principal lesson is that God created man as a free agent, and that the ills which are distinctively human owe their present existence, directly or remotely, to man's misuse of that supreme gift. The relevance of the story to men in all ages is emphasized by the fact that *Adam* is simply the Hebrew word for *man*. There is no man or woman living about whom this story is not a true story.

To turn to the modern scene, can we not see that the terror of war, the bitter disillusionment of an increasing number of broken homes, the growing inner insecurity of individuals all express the depth of the human predicament? Made for creative activity in harmony with their fellows and in unity with the purposes of the one true God, men have instead made themselves gods, with each man a competing center of activity and meaning, to the hurt of others, the destruction of his peace, and the frustration of his true destiny.

Obviously this problem has no simple solution (like more education or good resolutions), for the problem is not one of sins, to be conquered one by one, but of sin, a bent of mind and spirit, and a "warpedness" of society, which is too much for any one-by-one reform.

And for Our Salvation

THE fallen state of man does not alter God's love for us, but it obviously does alter the ways and means by which He can reach us to bring us to Himself. The Bible reveals God speaking to men through Law, Prophecy, and Wisdom, and then through our Lord Jesus Christ.[1] All reveal God's will for us. As our Lord summarized the law and the prophets: *Thou shalt love the Lord thy God with all thy heart, and with all thy soul . . . and with all thy mind; and thy neighbor as thyself.* But this is exactly what man, in his fallen state, cannot do. It is our profound humiliation that we cannot love either God or neighbor by mere obedience, mere resolution. So Jesus, as lawgiver, or even as example, is not enough. The crucial question is not, What is the right? but, How can I stand right with God when I have done wrong? It is in Jesus Christ that we find the answer to this question.

---

[1] For the story of this unfolding revelation see *The Holy Scriptures.*

The Apostles' Creed recites that Jesus Christ was conceived, born, suffered, was crucified, dead, and buried, rose again and ascended into heaven, and sits on the right hand of God. The Nicene Creed in a brief phrase defines the purpose of it all, *for us men and for our salvation*. As John Donne has said:

Everything that Christ said and did and suffered was for our salvation: As well His Mother wrapping Him in tiny clouts as Joseph wrapping Him in a winding sheet; as well His cold lying in the manger, as well His cold dying on the Cross.

So the one thing the Offices of Instruction say about the Son of God is that it is He *who hath redeemed me, and all mankind*.

WHY WE NEED SALVATION

REDEEMED—from what? From sin and death. These are the two realities that plague *me and all mankind* with a sense of guilt and with dread.

Sin is an unpopular word in many modern circles, but unfortunately what the word stands for has not been abolished. The fact is that men fail to meet God's high demand. That they ignore Him and His rôle as lawgiver does not change the fact, nor does it alter the consequences. Sin means separation from God, from fellow man, from one's true self. Throughout our culture community is broken, families are broken. Men also are broken within, and experience what Arnold Toynbee calls "schism in the soul." In our time, as talk about sin has decreased, there has been an increase of discussion about the guilt complex. Many who talk about and analyze this universal phenomenon still fail to see its most obvious explanation: that we have a sense of guilt because we are guilty. The Prayer Book (page 75) says of our sins, *The remembrance of them is grievous unto us; The burden of them is intolerable.*

Death also cannot be disposed of, nor forgotten. Men fear death, but they fear more what death implies: meaninglessness. The transience of things, insecurity, the prospect that our highest hopes and our greatest achievements will go down in the dust as do we ourselves, if they do not go down before—this is the bitterness in every cup of human joy.

The complacent man who denies experiencing either a sense of guilt or the reality of dread might learn something about himself if he consulted a psychoanalyst! For he would learn that much of his life consists of attempts to escape these inner fears. For he does feel these things—if not consciously, then in his depths. He would find that much of his life, including the most conventional activities and interests, are attempts to escape his inner fears. Therefore, anything that will save us from these twin evils will be salvation indeed.

Salvation—to what? The answer to these two difficulties —guilt and dread—is implied in their source. The guilt is due to sin. Sin is separation. Its cure is reconciliation. The dread is the prospect of death and meaninglessness. Its cure would be hope of eternal life and abiding purpose.

THE PROBLEM OF GUILT

How can we be rid of sin and guilt? Men have sought for this deliverance in many ways. First, they have tried to get rid of guilt by denying their sin. Some have said that there are no fixed moral laws. But their consciences have known better, and their sense of guilt has been dangerously suppressed rather than genuinely relieved. Some, even including Church members, have lowered God's demands in order to allow for easier performance, and therefore easier consciences, by reducing God's whole law to the Ten Commandments and a few added precepts of the Church. There are still more who reduce it simply to the code of polite society. But our Lord called for more than this. He called for the total allegiance of the whole person: *Thou shalt love the Lord thy God with all thy heart, and with all thy soul . . . and with all thy mind; and thy neighbor as thyself.* Anything less than this is sin. Some, assuming that God's demands were less than total, have tried to justify themselves by pious acts and other good deeds *over and above God's commandments . . . whereas Christ saith plainly, When ye have done all that are commanded to you, say, We are unprofitable servants.*[2]

We cannot reconcile ourselves to God by denying that there is a separation. *If we say that we have no sin, we deceive ourselves, and the truth is not in us. (I John 1:8.)* Nor can we reconcile ourselves to God by any merit on our part. *We have left undone those things which we ought to have done; And we have done those things which we ought not to have done; And there is no health in us.*[3] We have no extra merits with which to make up for our sins. Any good deeds we have done were expected of us. So it is obvious that if the gap between our sinful selves and the righteous God is to be bridged it must be bridged from His side.

That He did, and eternally does, just this through the Cross of Jesus Christ is the Good News of the Gospel: *God was in Christ, reconciling the world unto himself (II Co-*

---

[2] See the *Articles of Religion,* Article XIV.
[3] The General Confession in the Order for Daily Morning Prayer.

rinthians 5:19) and *God commendeth his love toward us, in that, while we were yet sinners, Christ died for us (Romans 5:8)*. In Christ, God has moved into our realm of life and has assumed the burden of our sinful flesh. In Christ, God has met us where we are. He has come down into human life to meet us in our desperate need. The Cross is not in the sky. It is planted in the earth. We have not been good enough to come to Him, so He has come to us. Nowhere does this truth become clearer than when at Communion we kneel and receive the broken bread and poured-out wine. As the familiar hymns (471 and 409) phrase it:

> *In my hand no price I bring,*
> *Simply to thy cross I cling.*

> *Just as I am, thy love unknown*
> *Has broken every barrier down.*

Certainly this has been the experience of Christians in all times and in all places. They have been found by Him in their deepest need, just as they were, without one plea. They have experienced the fact of being saved from sin and guilt.

THE MEANING OF THE CROSS

But why the Cross? Why did Jesus have to die for our sins? Would it not have been sufficient for Him to come among us and teach us about the mercies of God and the need for repentance? In the Cross, God was teaching us. But He was not only showing something to us, He was doing something for us.

What is it that He did?

We have been looking at the problem from man's direction. To see what it is that He has done, let us try to look at it from God's side. The problem, as traditional theology has expressed it, is how God can reconcile His justice and His mercy.

How can God reconcile His justice and His mercy? Confronted with man's sin He cannot say, "It doesn't matter; I don't care what you do." If He did that He would nullify the moral law, would belie His loving concern for us, would deny His own character. To do away with the moral law would thus be the cruelest thing God could do to men. It would mean that we did not matter to God. But, on the other hand, *If thou, Lord, wilt be extreme to mark what is done amiss, O Lord, who may abide it?* (Psalm 130:3). If the law is God's last word to us, then we all must be separated from Him forever, for all have sinned, all have broken God's law. If God is to be merciful, yet the law be maintained, then our redemption must be at a price. And since we have nothing to offer, He must take the hurt, pay the price.

We can understand this from a common human experience. If, for example, the wife of an errant husband were to say, "What you've done doesn't matter to me," she would do incalculable harm to the relationship. On the other hand, if she holds to the wrong of his act and will not forgive, she brings any real relationship to an end. She must find a way of upholding the meaning of family life with its unchanging obligations and yet forgive. This she does by looking beyond what he is to what he can be if they are reconciled. She maintains her standards and yet absorbs the hurt, takes it, and meets her repentant husband where he is, in love. She endures the sight of what he has been—that is, separated from her; and she does this for the sake of what he can be—that is, reunited with her. When he perceives that this is what she has done he is redeemed and loves her more than before. This is a human picture of what God has done for us in the Cross of Christ. This divine action is GRACE.

The Cross shows us that sin hurts. Sin matters. Yet the outstretched arms of the Crucified One bid us: *Come unto me, all . . . I will refresh you. (St. Matthew 11:28) . . . If I be lifted up, I will draw all men unto me (St. John 12:32) . . . So God loved the world, that he gave his only-begotten Son, to the end that all that believe in him should not perish (St. John 3:16).*

WHAT THE ATONEMENT IS

God was in Christ, reconciling the world to himself (II Corinthians 5:19). This mighty act of God for us men and for our salvation is known as THE ATONEMENT. In terms of each individual man's religious experience it is known as JUSTI-FICATION BY GRACE THROUGH FAITH: First, *justification:* that is, being taken for righteous. Secondly, *by grace:* that is, as a gift, as unmerited favor, not by the merit of one's own deeds. Thirdly, *through faith:* that is, received through the believer's response, through trust in Christ and commitment to Him, issuing in good works born of gratitude.

This definition points to man's part in the Atonement. True, the Atonement is primarily something which God does on our behalf, and we have emphasized this aspect of the matter. But there is more involved. First, in Christ, God is manifesting what He always has been and always will be: a righteous yet loving Father. This very revelation can elicit in man a response toward righteousness. Secondly, in Christ, God is showing what human life ought to be. Especially in the Cross do we see the supreme example of the sacrificial love for the brethren which is to be the hallmark of the disciple. Thirdly, on Calvary, Jesus as the perfect man, the one man completely obedient to the Father, interceded for us. Fourthly, since Jesus is true and representative man, He offered not only Himself but man to God. Since our Lord is one of us, we are by His Spirit enabled to join with Him in the eternal, once-for-all, offering He made and makes on our behalf. Finally, when in Christ, God entered our estate, healing came to our human nature. So while the primary fact about the Atonement is that God takes us for righteous though we are unrighteous, actually through the power of the Cross we become more righteous. Let us consider this process more closely.

THE FRUIT OF SALVATION

IF we are to be forgiven, three things must happen. We must examine our consciences and repent, we must have faith in God's forgiveness in Christ, and we must intend to amend our lives and keep God's law. Sören Kierkegaard has summarized it, "The profound humiliation of man, the boundless love of God, endless striving born of gratitude." This gratitude for salvation freely given, which is a stronger and more wholesome motive than the desire to earn salvation not yet attained, will gradually develop firmer habits of goodness in us. This activity is the human side of the gift of God known as SANCTIFICATION. *Justification by grace . . . through faith . . . unto good works (Ephesians 2:8-10)*. Grace is not only forgiveness, it is power to righteousness. But the law is still an absolute demand (*Be ye perfect*). New and more profound temptations await one on higher levels of performance, such as pride and complacency, and intolerance of others' weakness. Daily we repeat the cycle. Daily we examine and repent. Daily we receive God's forgiveness in faith. Daily we renew our grateful striving. We are continually saved by grace through faith unto good works.

In this way and this way alone can one face his shortcomings and know them for sin, yet feel at peace and confidently seek goodness. Otherwise one cannot be at peace because he cannot accept himself—unless he expects nothing of himself above what he is and does, or unless he pretends to righteousness. The sinner justified through Christ can accept himself as accepted by God though not deserving it. When he repents, with firm purpose of amendment, God accepts him. Hence he can accept himself and at the same time humbly see that on his own merits he was, and is, unacceptable. In accepting himself he takes his cue about himself from beyond himself. He knows that the last word about his sins is not that he has committed them but that they are forgiven. In this fashion all the important factors are preserved at one and the same time: honesty with one's self as to one's performance; peace with God, neighbor, and self; abiding joy and real ground for hope of improvement in one's performance day by day.

When our inner life can be so described, then surely our hearts will *there be fixed, where true joys are to be found.*[4] At no point in the cycle are we on the outside looking in. In St. Paul's frequently repeated phrase, we are in Christ. In this new life the sting of conscience does not abate, indeed it is sharpened—but even when we see our sins we are secure, for we know the source of forgiveness. It is Christ who does *abide in us and we in him* (*I John 4:13*).

---

[4] Prayer Book, page 174.

BUT man needs to be saved also from the dread of death and meaninglessness. By his own efforts, he can have even less hope of avoiding this fear than he might have of avoiding a sense of guilt. Notice how he tries to attribute abiding importance to his interests and hopes. See how he fails of satisfaction. This is especially evident in Western culture where competition has become a prevailing motive force in human life. In the nature of the case any achievement is always threatened by the greater achievement of others, and thus man sees the vanity of human enterprise. A man may laugh at all matters connected with death. He does this because humor is one of the ways of covering up a sense of insecurity. But he knows all the while that death is the only certain thing ahead for him. The answer to this need is obvious. He would no longer be in anxiety if he knew that his life had a place in the eternal scheme of things and that what he does now has abiding consequences for himself and for other men.

But man is finite. He can have eternal life only if he is given an opportunity to share in the life of him who is infinite. That he may do this is precisely the hope offered by the Risen Christ. The victory over the grave which the man Jesus experiences as God in man is offered to all men who will enter into His life. This is alike the life of the Cross and the life of resurrection.

THE RESURRECTION IS THE CHRISTIAN BELIEF

IN no Christian creed or confession of faith do we find the profession of belief in the immortality of the soul. What we do find is belief in the resurrection of the body from the dead. Just what this means is considered later. But here this much can be said. Unlike the Greek philosophers and those who have followed their way of thinking, we do not base our hope of eternal life primarily on the view that there is something inherent in human personality which is indestructible, that is, that the soul is by its very nature immortal. We have no assurance for such a view, save philosophical speculation. All that natural man can count on is death. But God, who is the power that implants life, can also restore life—as gift, and to whom He wills. Separated from God by our own acts of will and in rebellion from His law, we can count on nothing but what the eye readily sees. The body dies. Of any natural life apart from the body we have no evidence. And we know in the depths of conscience that our separation from God is precisely our sin, and that death and sin are inexorably linked together. Truly, *the wages of sin is death*.

Death is linked with sin. But so is the answer to death and sin. Who proclaims God's gift of resurrection? *Jesus Christ*. Who has broken down the barrier of our sins? *Jesus Christ*. He who offers the gift also makes it possible to receive it. Once His Cross has made possible the forgiveness of our sins, His resurrection can also be our resurrection. *The wages of sin is death?* Yes. *But the gift of God is eternal life through Jesus Christ our Lord.*

And Was Made Man

So to man in his sin and frustration, God comes in Christ with forgiveness and new life. By Christ and His Cross we are set free from our sin and released to the freedom which belongs to the sons of God. This is the plain truth of two thousand years of Christian experience. This is the central conviction of Christianity.

A story told about Sir James Simpson, the Scottish scientist who contributed largely to the development of surgical anaesthesia, sums it up. Asked one day by a student at Edinburgh, "Sir James, what do you consider your greatest discovery?" the surgeon, by this time an old man, replied quickly and with evident emotion, "That I am a great sinner and that Jesus Christ is a great Saviour." Here, surely, is authentic Christianity.

But if Jesus Christ does this, who can He be? For it is in that which Christ has done and still does, that we come to an understanding of who He was and still is. The fact of salvation demands that we have a doctrine about Christ adequate to explain what He has wrought in the lives of men. This can be seen in the New Testament itself. If, for example, we turn to the epistles of St. Paul, we shall see that it was through the experienced fact of St. Paul's own new life in Christ, that the Apostle came to see that he could not explain Jesus in any terms less than divinity.[1] It is the same with the rest of the New Testament. Every book in it builds its teaching about Jesus on the basic reality of the experienced forgiveness of God; of life in a new relationship or covenant with God and hence with one another. Each book asserts the gift of grace and the confidence of eternal life, both of which came to the first Christian believers through the redeeming work of our Lord.

ETHICS NOT CHRISTIANITY'S CENTRAL TEACHING

WE sometimes hear people say that after all the thing that matters about Christianity is its teaching that God is love, that we are to live as His children, and that we must be brotherly and sympathetic in our relations with our fellow men. However true these statements may be, and each of them is certainly true, they do not constitute the unique and special claim of the Christian faith. Statements like this can be paralleled in almost all kinds of religious teaching. But Christianity comes to us as Good News, not as a philosophical statement that God is our Father and all men are brethren. It comes to us as Good News of a fact which man could not learn by himself. The fact is that the eternal God *gave his only begotten Son, that whosoever believeth in him should not perish, but have everlasting life (St. John 3:16).*

Christianity is not defined adequately when it is simply

---

[1] See *The Holy Scriptures,* Chapter X.

called the religion that Jesus taught. It is rightly described only when it is seen as also the Gospel proclaiming what God has done in Jesus for the salvation of the world. In other words, it is a faith centering in Jesus, in what He has done and in who He is. We come to know who He is as we contemplate and experience what He has done.

WHAT THE CHURCH SAYS ABOUT CHRIST

THE Christian Church has made three assertions of a theological nature about Christ:

The first is that Jesus Christ is divine. He is very God of very God.

The second is that Jesus Christ is human. He is very man.

The third is that in Jesus Christ God and man are brought together in such a unique and wonderful way that He may properly be called the one Person who is God and man, united "unchangeably, unconfusedly, indivisably, and inseparably."

Unless these assertions are true, there can be no adequate explanation of Christianity at all. Unless they are accepted and experienced to be true, none of us can enter into the richness and the fullness of the Christian life. The fundamental distinction between historic Christianity and all those reduced and minimizing versions of Christianity which have appeared at one time or another is right here. Christ is not merely a human teacher and prophet. He is supremely the coming of God to man, a coming whose result is a new relationship to God available to us in no other way.

This is the reason that the New Testament calls Him Lord. In the days of primitive and early Christianity, this term was employed to describe one who was truly divine.

It was used as a name for God in the Old Testament. It was applied to the deities worshipped by the Gentiles. When, therefore, Jesus is called Lord, this means that Christian believers know Him to be so much more than a man that they must seek out and employ the highest terms available to them and apply such terms to Him who, as the early believers said, *brought life and immortality to light* (*II Timothy 1:10*). The New Testament shows that its writers knew that Jesus had saved them from their sins. He had brought them out of darkness into the light. Only God could do that. And while Jesus Christ indubitably was a man, He was on God's side of the division which man's sin had set up between God and man. He was their Leader and Master. But He was even more, He was their Lord, supreme over all human leaders and masters because He had *come from God*.

Furthermore, when the first Christians spoke of Jesus as the Son of God, they did not intend to equate Him with other men who are sons of God. Jesus was *the* Son, in a sense quite different from that in which Peter and Paul and Timothy were sons. The whole history of the doctrine of Christ may well be regarded as the attempt to understand what this difference in sonship between Jesus and the rest of us means. And this is why no Christian can be content to reduce the unique and special sonship of Jesus (which is what *his only Son* means in the creeds), to the general sonship which all of us have. Indeed, the great distinction is demonstrated by the plain fact that for those who have known the redemption wrought in Christ, the general sonship to God which all men have is replaced by a share in Christ's special sonship. That is why St. Paul, for example, can speak of our becoming *sons of God* through Christ. So overwhelmingly different from our broken relationship with God before Christ came and did His saving work is our relationship with God after Christ.

In this chapter we shall endeavor to expound the three assertions made about Christ:

Jesus is truly divine.

Jesus is truly human.

Jesus is one person who is God and man.

But because manhood is so much more readily understandable than deity or Godhead to us who are men, we shall start with the second of the affirmations and then return to the first.

THE HUMANITY OF CHRIST

It should be perfectly plain to anyone who reads the Gospels that Jesus Christ lived a human life. Although the early Church was obliged to face and defeat a denial of this truth,[2] no one today would suppose that the manhood of Christ was a disguise or a masquerade or an appearance with no reality in it. Jesus was really born. He grew up as a boy and young man. He walked the lanes and highways of the Holy Land. He ate and drank and talked and listened. He knew human emotion—witness His weeping over Jerusalem and its people. He delighted in human companionship. He suffered pain. The misunderstandings of His people were real to Him, as were the anguish and pain which He bore on the Cross. He died as all men die.

It is indeed true that He rose from the dead, victorious over death itself; but that triumph is not the negation of death but the conquest of it. There cannot be the slightest doubt that in every way Jesus was man.

---

[2] *Chapters in Church History,* pages 34 ff.

In Him there was that positive goodness, that perfect obedience to the Father's will, that total surrender to God and His purpose, which brought His human nature to absolute perfection. In meeting temptation at the beginning of His ministry, Jesus committed Himself to the Father's will. And in the Garden of Gethsemane His commitment is made complete: *Not my will, but thine, be done* (*St. Luke 22:42*). If we want to see what man is meant to be, we must look at Jesus. This is manhood at its best, completely fulfilling all that manhood is intended to be.

He was sinless. Yet the fact that Jesus appears to us in the Gospels as sinless does not detract from His full and true humanity. For, as we have seen in chapter IV, sin is not an essential part of human nature. It is a disease that is so pervasive and universal that we rightly say that "all men are sinners." But Jesus Christ is the exception here. In Him, as St. John tells us, there was no sin. This is true man. We are not true men, for we are in terrible defection from the norm. We are sinners and belong to a race of sinners. Jesus is the New Adam, in St. Paul's phrase. He is man in God's image, perfect as His Father is perfect.

The Christian Church has, accordingly, always asserted uncompromisingly that Jesus Christ is man, *bone of our bone, flesh of our flesh*. There have been Christians, down the ages, who in their proper desire to emphasize the deity of Jesus have tended to slight the balancing fact of His manhood. But against these individual thinkers or writers, the common sense of the Church has spoken with conviction. The Nicene Creed has always stood as the guarantee of the fact which the title of this chapter takes from that Creed, that God *was made man*.

It is this double truth that the phrases *conceived by the*

86

Holy Ghost, born of the Virgin Mary were intended to affirm.

The Church's tradition has been that Christ was born of a virgin, but this has never been intended as a denial of His full humanity. The basis of this tradition is in the Gospels of St. Matthew and St. Luke. The Church has always insisted on the theological meaning of the creedal statement about the birth of Jesus—namely, that He is a new creation, *conceived by the Holy Ghost*.[3] He is God's new initiative in human life, His humanity being related to God in a unique and special way.

Now, to be a man one must live in a particular place and at a particular time and under particular conditions. One cannot be a man in a generalized sort of way. One must be a man in a particular way. This is inevitable if there is to be a true Incarnation. So Jesus was born and lived and died under the circumstances described in the Gospels. He was a Jew, whose native land was Palestine. He lived in the first few decades of what we call our era. His conditions of life, the circumstances in which He was man, were those of late Judaism.

But there is more than that to the truth of manhood. If there is to be a real man, it is necessary that there be not only a human body, human emotions, human experience in a physical sense. It is also necessary that there be a human mind, human thought, human experience in an intellectual sense. This, too, the Church has asserted about Jesus.

In the discussion in *Chapters in Church History* (pages

---

[3] There is no disagreement within the Church on the theological meaning of the Virgin Birth. We recognize that some have difficulty as to the historical account. See the Books for Reference, page 203, for treatments of this subject.

33-38) of the heresies which plagued the Church during the first three centuries, attention was given to the erroneous views of those whose mistake was that they could not believe that Christ did in fact possess a human mind. They felt that it was unfitting that God, in becoming man, should have known the limitations which are involved in human thought. So they said that instead of a human mind, Jesus had as the intellectual and spiritual center of His human existence, the divine mind, the Word or *Logos*. But with a sure instinct the Church condemned this theory as entirely false. For it knew, as St. Athanasius said, that if God did not take to himself a human mind as well as a human body, then the most important element in man has not been redeemed at all. For we do not sin as bodies alone; we sin as minds which use bodies. We fail to do God's will because our minds are opposed to God's will, not because our bodies are evil.

Surely the Church was altogether right in saying this. Our ordinary experience makes us all understand that it is by our choosing, our willing, our desiring, that we fall short of the standard which God has set for us. The wonderful thing about the manhood of our Lord is that while His human mind was like ours, with the limitations that ours also possess, it was a human mind entirely at one with God, choosing and willing and desiring what God willed, and not seeking to have its own way. There was perfect accord between the human mind of Jesus and the purpose of God.

On the other hand, because the human mind of Jesus was a genuine human mind, there were things which that mind could not know. This is evident in the Gospels. Jesus Himself said that there were things which He did not know, but which were known only to the Father.[4] Furthermore, because the mind of Jesus, humanly speaking, was the mind of a Jew of the first century, He naturally shared many of the ideas which were current at that time. He thought, for example, that David wrote all the Psalms,[5] although we have since learned (through the study of the biblical evidence) that many of them were not written by David. Every Jew in our Lord's time believed that David was their author. How could Jesus have been truly human if His human mind had not been thus conditioned?

THE AUTHORITY OF JESUS' TEACHING

Now the fact that the human mind of Jesus was limited in this way, should not for a moment lead us to suppose that on the crucial and essential issues of human life our Lord thought as other Jews of His time. For what are the crucial and essential concerns of human life? Are they not man's relation to God, his relation to his human brethren, the purpose for which he was created, and the destiny which awaits him in the future? On these matters Jesus' mind was not limited by current Jewish ideas. Because He and the Father were one, He knew, with a directness and certainty which could come only from the inspiration of God Himself, from the Holy Spirit given to Him without measure, that man is created in God's image and for God.

Man is to live in childlike humility and faith, in love and charity with his brethren, fulfilling his calling by reflecting the divine purpose of love, and destined to live in God's presence to all eternity. Here Jesus speaks with authority, as from God.

---

[4] St. Mark 13:32.
[5] Compare His statement on Psalm 110 found in St. Mark 12:36.

Furthermore, on matters which result from these central truths, Jesus thought and spoke with moral inerrancy. His moral teaching is not merely an opinion about what constitutes the good life for man. It springs from and it illuminates the nature of man as God has made him. It is ultimate and final law for man. We are to be just, righteous, forgiving, compassionate, because as Jesus knew so clearly, we are God's children and must live as brethren under God.[6]

It is on points like these that we can see that the human mind of Jesus, although like ours in its limitations, was unlike ours in its fullness of insight and its profound grasp of the essential truth about life.

THE MIGHTY WORKS OF JESUS

WE read in the Gospels that Jesus did many mighty works. He healed the sick. He raised the dead. He stilled the storm. The problem presented by these and other miracles is very real for numbers of people. No treatment of the Christian faith can avoid facing it. This is an appropriate place to comment briefly on this matter.

We must first of all recognize that the concept of the miraculous guards an essential truth about God's relation to the world which He has created and which at every moment He sustains. The kind of God in whom Christians believe is not bound by any rigid laws of a mechanical sort. He is a free being. He acts within His world, shaping it according to His will as by His Spirit He works through it to awaken a free response. The only necessity laid upon God comes through His own choosing.

---

[6] A fuller discussion of the meaning of Jesus' teaching will appear in a subsequent volume in this series.

Hence, when scientists discover uniformities in nature, they are "thinking God's thoughts after Him." He made the world in such a way that it does not continue in a haphazard fashion but follows a plan. Yet no scientist can prescribe what shall or shall not happen. He can only observe what has in fact already happened and tabulate a series of events which have followed more or less consistently a particular line. Oxygen and hydrogen, in a certain combination, have always produced water. This does not mean that any arbitrary law makes this happen, but rather that this is the way it has observably always happened. God wills it shall be so.

But the world is an open world, where really new things do take place. The beginning of creation itself was a new act. The Christian believes that God can do something new without contradicting any of the findings of science, since the latter are always retrospective.

No human mind can prescribe exactly what was or was not possible for Jesus Christ who was in the unique position of being both God and man. Nevertheless, we do know that Christ always must have acted consistently with the divine character and purpose of holiness and love. He always must have acted as man, since He is by definition of faith God-Man. If He were only a man like ourselves, we should not expect Him to have performed mighty acts. Since He was more than that, we are prepared to believe that He exceeded the possibilities of ordinary human nature.

For example, we should expect Him to have met human illness with healing, for He was compassionate and the lover of men.

The most important point, however, in any discussion

of the miraculous is to keep hold of the truth that God can and does act consistently, yet in new and unexpected ways. Much that happens we cannot understand, since our human minds are limited and our human vision imperfect. There are many more things in the world than a secular thinker would allow.

Furthermore, the Church maintains that God in Christ accomplished a new creation, in which all His creatures may find redemption. This in itself is miraculous, since nothing in our human understanding could predict its occurrence. It is of God's free grace that Christ came and delivered us from sin. Christ Himself is the great miracle. The miracles reported about Him in the Gospels are an expression of the overwhelming reality of God made flesh and dwelling among us, full of grace and truth.

Finally, it is within the Christian fellowship of faith and worship that men come to see the meaning of the miraculous element in life. Through loyal participation in its whole life men will enter more deeply into the experience which includes the miracle of redemption. Within that experience they will come to understand the significance and point of the historical miracles of the gospels.

THE DEITY OF CHRIST

THE proclamation of the Christian Church is, then, that Jesus of Nazareth who *was mighty in word and deed*, the perfect man, is also true God. He comes to us from God. As the Nicene Creed declares, He is *God of God, Light of Light, Very God of very God.*[7]

Because of what He has done, in redeeming us from sin

---

[7] The Greek and Latin of these phrases make their meaning clearer: God *from* or *out of* God. Christ is *God sent from God.*

and opening to us *the gate of everlasting life,* He must be more than man, even than man at his best. Indeed it is terribly true that, without Christ's redeeming work, His teaching about God and our human duty is in a deep sense bad news, not good. If Jesus had merely taught us an impossible law, the rule of love toward God and man, He would have mocked us. Jesus as Teacher was the climax of the Law. But law cannot save us, as St. Paul rightly asserted. To have only the knowledge of what God demands makes us despair. What we need is divine *grace and power faithfully to perform* His demands. Jesus the Redeemer, by His saving action completed on Calvary and vindicated by the Resurrection, makes this grace and power available for every man. Therefore when we are confronted by Jesus, we are not moved to applaud a great human achievement, as if He were the greatest man among men. We know rather, that we must fall on our knees before One who though He is of our flesh is yet our Lord and Saviour. We are like St. Thomas who cried out, when he saw his Lord risen from the dead, *My Lord and my God.*

The Christian Church has never hesitated to make this bold assertion. It has declared that in Jesus, God has not only visited but has redeemed His people. God has come to us in Jesus. He has come in human terms, which we can understand; He has come as a brother man, whom we can love. He has come. God is here, in Jesus.

How different this is from the thought that in Christ there is a kind of impersonal divinity! How removed it is from the idea that He is an "incarnation of moral and religious values and truths." In Him is truth, of course. But no personification of moral and religious ideas could ever redeem men from their sin and unite them with God. If

Jesus be divine at all, He must be as God is. He must, in-deed, be God himself. Nothing less than this will do.

The early Church, which was obliged to face so many false theories and so many inadequate explanations of Christ, was for many years confronted with attempts to describe Christ in ways which would have lowered or re-duced His deity or Godhead. It rejected these attempts, one after another, until finally at Nicaea in 325 the Church pro-claimed the great truth which is in our Nicene Creed: He is *of one substance with the Father*. The term *substance* meant, for the Fathers of the Church, approximately what *fundamental reality* means today. To say, therefore, that Christ is *of one substance with the Father* is to say that in Him we meet the same fundamental reality which is in God the Creator.

This assertion is no mere speculative matter; it is ra-tionally necessary for the truth of the story of man's salva-tion in Christ. If Jesus were merely a good man or an archangel or some strange being *like* God, then we might think that God had let someone other than Himself suffer for our sins. In that case the Cross would remain a model of sacrifice for an ideal, but it could not show God's love. Men would still have to stand ignorant before the great question: Does God care? And they would not have the *joy and peace in believing (Romans 15:13)* which comes with the knowledge that God Himself has entered our hu-man life and in that life has Himself wrought our salvation. It is for this reason, so essential to living the Gospel-faith, that the Church has never been content with any reduced divinity in the person of the Lord Jesus Christ. Rather, it has unswervingly declared that our Lord who brings us to our knees before Him, who saves us from our sin and

94

unites us with our heavenly Father, is truly divine. He is *Very God of very God,* who for us men and for our salvation has come down from heaven, and has been made man.

Someone has said that this is the scandalous assertion of the Christian Gospel. And so it is. For scandalous means that which causes men to stumble. And this is what Christianity most certainly does. It makes claims that offend self-satisfied, narrowly rational men. Its assertion is not that God is good; its claim is that we know He is good because He has become man, to make us whole and to set us free.

We cannot explain this, any more than we can explain a great many other mysteries by which our human life is surrounded and in the midst of which we spend our days. If we cannot explain the union of two persons in marriage, a union in which they live in each other and know each other with a complete and wonderful knowledge; if we cannot explain human friendship; if we cannot explain, in a nice and precise way, most of the things that make life worthwhile . . . how can we hope to explain the mystery of God made man? We can only accept this mystery and then let God lead us into a deeper knowledge of the Incarnate Lord.

THE PERSONAL UNION OF GOD AND MAN IN CHRIST

THE Christian affirmation is that the almighty God is so united with manhood in Jesus Christ that the union can never be broken. It is a union so intimate, direct, complete, that we call it a personal union. The directing principle in the life of Jesus Christ is not just a human mind or soul as it is in us. Although our Lord certainly possessed both human mind and soul, it is God himself who directs and governs the whole life of Jesus Christ. Or, to make a precise theological statement, it is the Second Person of the Holy and Undivided Trinity, the Eternal Son, who created and took human nature in the womb of Mary, uniting Himself with that nature indivisibly, inseparably, unconfusedly, unchangeably.[8] God and man are so much at one in Jesus, that we cannot properly talk about this union as a mere juxtaposition of God and man. The Church has affirmed that Jesus Christ is One Person in two natures: God and man in Him are one in the fullest sense. This is a mystery. Yet it is the ground of all Christianity and the heart of our faith.

Unless this be true, the basis for the Christian life itself is imperiled. If He is not truly man, then He cannot be for us the pattern of manhood. If He is not truly God, He could not bring God to us and save us from sin, since only God can forgive the one who has offended against Him. If He is not truly the personal union of God and man, then He has not accomplished for us the salvation which we as Christians know that He has in very deed worked out for us. That is the deliverance of Christian experience. The stories of the birth of Jesus, which tell us that the divine act preceded the human response, make this clear. The Creed puts this in the words *conceived by the Holy Ghost, Born of the Virgin Mary*. Jesus was not just another man, however good. He was God come as man, born of a woman to redeem all men.

Consider by way of illustration how an acquaintance with whom we have been on formal terms may in an emergency act with extraordinary helpfulness and with a strong desire to assist us in our trouble. So with God. With Him

---

[8] These are the adverbs used at Chalcedon in A.D. 451 to describe the union of God and Man in Christ. Compare the discussion in *Chapters in Church History*, page 37.

we men have been on formal, more or less friendly, more or less unfriendly, terms. And then comes Jesus, in whom God acts in a new way, assisting us in our need, setting us on the right path, releasing us from the fear that we had no one on whom we could count and in whom we could trust.

Of course God is not confined to Jesus. God by His eternal Word is universally present, everywhere active, laboring incessantly to bring us to Himself, always revealing something of His character and purpose. But such a general disclosure and activity of God's nature cannot save us.

What we need is the concentration, the intensification, of God's presence and action and revelation, so that it strikes home vividly and unmistakably. This is what God has done in Christ. It is true that the Word of God is the very ground of every human life. He it is in whom our existence is rooted. If His life-giving presence were withdrawn from us, we would wither and die. It also is true that in holy people, the saints and seers and prophets, we see God at work in a special way. But in Jesus Christ, Christians declare, something different has happened. He has created one instance of human life, brother to each of us and so "of our substance." He has possessed Himself of that life in such a direct and immediate way, that we cry out, "This is God with us as man." [9]

Many of us will remember that as children we used to play with a magnifying glass, taking it out into the sunlight

[9] As the reader may have noted, this discussion prepares for the Church's declaration that God is Trinity-in-Unity. We have talked about God the Father; about the meaning of Christ, who is God the Son; and by implication about the work of God the Holy Ghost. In Chapter VIII there will be a more complete presentation of the work of the Holy Ghost. Then in the final chapter we shall see how the full Christian teaching about God includes all this in God as the Holy Trinity.

and catching the rays in the lens. The sun's rays were not confined to the glass. They were shining down everywhere in the garden, causing the grass to grow, giving light and color to the walks and the flowers, bringing the warmth of a summer's day to our parents and friends and to our own young bodies. But as we caught the rays in that lens, focusing them there, something new and wonderful happened. When a piece of paper or a cloth was placed beneath the glass, the concentration of the rays was so intense that it set the paper or the cloth on fire. So we may say that God is indeed present everywhere, working everywhere, bringing life and light, warmth and healing, to the whole world and to every man. All that is required of man is that he open his life to God. But it is just this that man cannot do, of himself, for he is a sinner. It is only God who can turn us to Himself. This He has done in Jesus Christ. He has so focused and concentrated His presence and His work in this man Jesus Christ that when others are exposed to Him there, they too are set on fire. And the fire is the interacting love to God and to men which flames up when we are touched by the love of God Himself which is in Christ Jesus our Lord.

He Rose . . . He Ascended . . . He Shall Come to Judge

IF the Cross were the final symbol of the love of God shown us in Christ, we should indeed believe in His goodness but we should doubt His power. We should be compelled to see at the heart of the universe, and as its final meaning, tragedy, not triumph. If we truly believe that God is in Christ, then a Christ for whose life the last chapter is death spells a God who in the ultimate test is defeated. Yet if there were a single word which could characterize the dominant mood of the early Christians it would be Triumph. This was because they believed in the victory of their Lord over death; the RESURRECTION was at the heart of their thought and devotion.

WHY WE BELIEVE IN CHRIST'S RESURRECTION

THERE is no more convincing argument for belief in the Resurrection[1] than the existence of the Christian Church.

---

[1] See *The Holy Scriptures,* pages 147-48.

It is not on Calvary that we find Jesus' disciples. The contemplation of its outcome led one to betray Him. Its nearness caused another to deny Him. And its event put the remainder to flight. But after the disciples were convinced that they had seen the Risen Lord they preached this conviction with boldness, each preparing the way for his own Calvary, confident that he would share with Christ in His Resurrection. In turn the power this brought to their lives was so contagious that thousands, who heard the simple straightforward account from the eye-witnesses, themselves believed, and were themselves put in touch with the Living Christ. The power of their changed lives reached still others. Thus the process repeated itself from town to town, from nation to nation, from generation to generation, from century to century until today there are more believers in the Resurrection of Christ than at any previous time in history. Every Sunday we are reminded of the fact that the Church is here because Christ rose from the dead. Pious Jews, steeped in thousands of years of tradition, changed their day of worship from the old Sabbath to the new Sunday, the day of the Resurrection. What is now the name of a monastic order in the Church of England could well be used to describe the Christian Church throughout the centuries: *The Community of the Resurrection*.

The Church is built on the faith that Jesus rose victorious over the grave.

Not merely did His memory abide; not merely did His principles or His teachings abide; He abides. The disciples were with Him, as persons with a person. Did He have a physical body? Obviously He had some body. It is certain that He had a form through which His spirit could be in communication with others. The exact nature of this body the New Testament record leaves unsettled, some passages making one assumption, some the other. This is a matter more conveniently discussed in chapter XI in connection with the article of the Creed *I believe in . . . The Resurrection of the body*. The precise kind of body is not the important thing. The important thing is the fact that Jesus Christ was known and experienced as a real person in genuine communication with those who responded to Him in faith.

THE ASCENSION

THE Christian religion is not a body of religious principles but faith in the mighty acts of God. This is testified to by the fact that the Creeds include one verb after another in the past tense: *conceived . . . born . . . suffered . . . crucified . . . died . . . was buried . . . rose again.* Then we have one more verb in the past tense followed by a present: *He ascended into Heaven, And* sitteth *on the right hand of God.* "It is," says Karl Barth, "as if we had made the ascent of a mountain and had now reached its summit." THE ASCENSION is the affirmation of the eternal character of God's victory in Christ.

We must not be put off by difficulties of celestial geography. To be sure, the terms in which the experience of the Apostles is reported are not in accord with Copernican astronomy. Believing in a three-layer universe, the first Christians naturally assumed, upon Christ's disappearance from them at the end of His earthly manifestations, that He went up. In any event, His Resurrection appearances came to an end and He entered the eternal realm. Even more obviously metaphorical is the phrase *sitteth on the right hand of God.* In some places the Creed reads "at the left hand of God," the left hand being the place of honor in some cultures.

Such words aim to express in more vivid terms what the prologue to St. John's Gospel expresses more philosophically: *In the beginning was the Word, and the Word was with God, and the Word was God.* Christ is the eternal Word. He is to God as word is to idea, and word and idea are not separate things.

THE MEANING OF THE RESURRECTION
AND THE ASCENSION

In spite of the difficulty of expressing such eternal concepts, the Church has always proclaimed as fundamentals of the faith the Ascension of Christ and the Resurrection of which it is the climax. Here are essential truths about God and about our Christian life.

First, they mean that God is eternally in all that Jesus Christ manifested to us in His earthly life, all that He did for us in His atoning death, all that is promised to us by His rising from the dead. *Once-for-all* is the phrase we use to emphasize the historical character of these mighty acts and the fact that they need not, will not, be repeated. But the *for all* is just as important in the phrase as the *once*, and the Resurrection and the Ascension stand for the fact that the power of Christ's saving and restoring acts is available, unabated, to men in any century. This is because in Christ we do not see played out on the human stage an exception to God's behavior. We see revealed in Christ what God eternally is, we see Him acting characteristically. Ours is a God who ever judges, but He is also One *whose nature and property is ever to have mercy and to forgive.*

Secondly, the Resurrection and Ascension mean that

Christ is King. He has a Kingdom. It is one which inter-penetrates the nations of this world. Its subjects are found under every flag. He told His disciples, *The Kingdom of Heaven is in your midst;* and so it has been in our midst ever since. His reign is in the hearts of those who belong to the fellowship of faith. This invisible kingdom has visi-ble manifestations, not only in the visible Church but also working as a leaven within the whole of society.

The Kingdom is not a name used to describe a fellowship of those who treasure the principles of some long-dead leader. He who is the source of its meaning is also its living Leader, who ever reigns over it, *Wherefore God also hath highly exalted him, and given him a name which is above every name: That at the name of Jesus every knee should bow, of things in heaven, and things in earth, and things under the earth; And that every tongue should confess that Jesus Christ is Lord, to the glory of God the Father (Philippians 2:9-11).* Truly it is He, in the words of the Nicene Creed, *Whose kingdom shall have no end.*

Thirdly, the Ascension means that manhood, glorified, has an eternal place in the life of God. Thus the persisting value of our manhood is affirmed. An old prayer, used in the Latin eucharistic rite as the wine and water are poured in the chalice (the wine and water traditionally symbolizing the divine and human natures of Christ), runs:

O God, by whom the dignity of human nature was won-drously established and yet more wondrously restored, grant, that by the mystery signified in the mingling of this water and wine, we may partake of His divinity who did partake of our humanity, namely, Jesus Christ, thy Son, our Lord, who liveth and reigneth with thee in the unity of the Holy Ghost, world without end.

Because of Christ we know that we have a place in the eternal realm. *Seeing then that we have a great high priest, that is passed into the heavens, Jesus the Son of God, . . . let us therefore come boldly unto the throne of grace (Hebrews 4:14, 16)*, through Jesus Christ our Lord *in whom we have boldness and confidence of access through our faith in him (Ephesians 3:12 RSV)*.

THE SECOND COMING OF CHRIST

WE have seen that in *sitteth on the right hand of God* we reach a summit. Now it is as though we look beyond, on the other side to the horizon, *He shall come*. Time and history, this world, will come to an end. It may be by God's doing or it may be by man's doing, in the exercise of the freedom God has given him (for example, by atomic fission). However it happens, a new world is coming, not as something achieved from this side, but as something given from the other side. At the end of human history stands THE JUDGMENT.

Who is he that will come to judge? He who has already come. This determines the character of the judgment. We know Him whom we have to face. And thus we know the standards by which we shall be judged. As man, He knows what men can do. He is *touched with the feeling of our infirmities*, and thus understands our human limitations. But He also knows our possibilities. Indeed, in His own life He fully realized them. The fact that He is one of us promises a fair and understanding, but also a rigorous and definite judgment. Our Lord *was in all points tempted like as we are, yet without sin (Hebrews 4:15)*. This text presents the two aspects of the Judge whom we shall have to face: *We have not an high priest which cannot be touched*

*with the feeling of our infirmities; yet all things are naked
and opened unto the eyes of him with whom we have to do*
(*Hebrews 4:13*).

THE JUDGMENT IS NOW

WHEN will be the judgment? At the end of time. But while
time shall come to an end, eternity does not just then begin.
We are at present in life eternal. The meaning of the eternal realm is defined in the familiar response in the *Gloria
Patri: As it was in the beginning, is now, and ever shall be,
world without end.* In Christ, the eternal Word was incarnate in temporal life, Christ became involved in time
and history and remains so involved until the end of time
and history. He is at the intersection of time and eternity.
The end of time is where He is. Thus the judgment is not
simply future. It broods over history. It stands as the measure of each individual life, indeed of each individual
thought, word, deed, or omission. The judgment is now.
Christ was judge from the time of His coming. The fore-
runner, St. John the Baptist, said of Him, *His winnowing-
fan is in his hand, he will clean out his threshing-floor* (*St.
Matthew 3:12.* Moffatt).

The author of St. John's Gospel selects as the first in-
cident of our Lord's ministry the cleansing of the temple.
The first coming and His second coming form two pillars
of an arch which stands over all the time that is between.
Past and future. They determine the nature of the present.
The time will come when all things will be made manifest.
But meanwhile, in this interim between the two comings,
things are even now being made manifest. Life is being
judged, the true nature of intentions and actions is known.
So in this sense the judgment is now. *If the householder*

had known at what watch in the night the thief was coming, he would have been on the watch, he would not have allowed his house to be broken into (St. Matthew 24:43. Moffatt). When the author comes on stage, the play is over.

THE CHRISTIAN UNDERSTANDING OF HISTORY

MEANWHILE, then, we live in an interim age, *until He comes again.* His Kingdom has come, yet is to come. In the same prayer we say *Thine is the kingdom,* having just prayed *Thy kingdom come.* This is the core of the Christian interpretation of the meaning of history. Of course this is a most difficult subject, about which many volumes have been written, especially in the past few years. It is hardly a new theme. *The Book of Revelation* in the New Testament and St. Augustine's *City of God* are classic treatments of the subject. Difficult as it is to state the Christian understanding of history, it is necessary in this chapter to discuss it briefly.

There are three ways of relating history to the final meaning of things. One way is to say that only the eternal realm matters. This life and this world are unimportant in themselves. They serve only as a vestibule to the main room, only as a place and period of preparation. This otherworldly approach is typical of oriental religions, but Christianity has sometimes been presented in a way which approximates it.

A second approach is to say that temporal history is the final and only realm of meaning. This is the basic premise of *secularism,* which is a word deriving from *saeculum,* age. It is this-age-ism. All secularists would agree that whatever meaning there is in historical experience is in this world. Some of them would disclaim any meaning at all.

Other secularists would claim that there is a meaning. For many old-fashioned liberals, for example, it is the doctrine of human progress. For the Marxists, it is the inevitability of the class struggle and the ultimate victory of the proletariat.

The third approach is to say there is meaning in both the eternal realm and the historical realm. The Christian Church has affirmed this teaching. This world does matter, but it is not the source of its own power and meaning. What happens here has meaning for two reasons. First, the development of creative personalities, sound personal relations, constructive community life, and a peaceful world are in themselves valuable. They are part of the very object of creation. They are ways in which man, made in God's image, can share in God's creative activity and, in a sense, help finish His creation—help reduce chaos to order. A well-built house, a lovely park, a joyous family gathering, sound labor-management relations in a factory, the breakdown of racial intolerance in a community, a great religious procession, the sunlight caught on a canvas—all these are ends, worthwhile for their very beauty and order and justice and for what they mean to the personality of man. But they are also means to another end. What happens here matters because abiding consequences hinge on decisions made here. Here is where men turn toward God or away from Him. Here there are real means of grace. Here men can be saved. This world is doubtless not the only place where grace can reach men. Nor is it the only place where men can respond to grace. But it is a place and the only place in which we can directly function now and the one we know the most about. It is the place where we are responsible for faithful action now.

WHAT then is progress? Certainly those who see history in the biblical perspective know that nations and cultures rise and fall, and that the building of bigger and better things does not as such mean anything. It is people who matter and who have eternal destiny. And people can in the worst times receive grace, while people in the most favorable times can reject it. Yet some conditions, spiritual and material, make men more meet than other conditions to receive grace. So here is the realm where there can be real progress, where the eternal is functioning in and through the temporal. There can be a progressive increase in the means of grace.

Thus it is equally wrong to say this world is the Kingdom, or to say that it is not the Kingdom. Rather, in the words of Arnold Toynbee, this world is a "province of the Kingdom of God," one of the realms in which the Kingdom operates. The progress of this world can be measured by the degree to which the means of grace for men are ever increasing in it. Here we Christians are *colonists of Heaven* (*Philippians 3:20*. Moffatt). Obviously, then, the Church must *preach the gospel to every creature.* The whole Church is a missionary society. The Church must manifest an active and imaginative social concern, to make the world increasingly a place in which men can recognize the hand of God, and the power of His Christ, *Whose kingdom shall have no end.*

The Holy Ghost, The Lord, and Giver of Life

OF all the articles in the Creed, the one about the Holy Spirit or Holy Ghost is probably the least understood by Church people. It is certainly the one least understood by the man or woman outside the Church. When one speaks about school spirit or the spirit of fellowship, he is usually understood. But when one speaks of the Holy Spirit, communication breaks down. Yet the Holy Spirit is constantly with us, supporting us, strengthening us, guiding us; and such a conviction is fundamental to a sound and basic Christianity. Perhaps one reason many do not recognize the Holy Spirit is that He speaks to us chiefly about Christ, and not about Himself. Nevertheless, failure to understand who He is and what He does is responsible for much of the confusion in our religious thinking. Failure to respond to His presence and power has made much of our contemporary Christianity impotent.

Most of us are fairly sure of what we mean when we use spirit with a small "s." Take, for example, the familiar expression "the spirit of America." Presumably for most of us this means that we are bound together in a national unity, in loyalty to common ideals and aims. It means that we participate in a common heritage. As patriots we are impelled to obey an inner drive toward coöperation with our fellows and to recognize the claims of our nation upon us. We share, often with sacrificial cost, its way of life and are ready to defend that way to the death. The spirit of America takes possession of us, compels us, urges us, persuades us, inspires us. It helps us to be good citizens of our land.

Now the Holy Spirit means much more than this. The Church affirms that the Holy Spirit is personal, like God the Father and the Eternal Son, Jesus Christ our Lord. He is no vague, impersonal, diffused influence. We speak of the Holy Spirit as *he* not *it;* He is a personal, active, and living reality. You could not say that about the spirit of America. This is precisely where the analogy breaks down.

THE HOLY SPIRIT IN THE EARLY CHURCH

THERE are, it is true, many things which we say about the Holy Spirit that are not unlike the statements we make about the spirit. Go back to the first days of the Christian Church. Jesus Christ had come among men, teaching, preaching, healing, performing mighty acts. He had gathered His band of followers and companied with them day by day. He had attacked those Jewish leaders who had perverted their religion and He had therefore been arrested, tried, crucified. He had risen from the dead and had made Himself known *by many infallible proofs (Acts 1:3)*.

What happened then? As a result of this total experience the disciples and their converts found themselves possessed by a new spirit, a spirit of fellowship, a spirit of power, a spirit of love. But here is the real difference. This spirit known to the Christians was so authoritative, so compelling, so demanding of obedience, that men followed wherever they were led; so personal in operation, that the early Christians knew that the spirit was *The Spirit*. They identified Him with the Spirit about whom they had read in their Scriptures. He was the same Spirit who had come mightily upon men of old. He was the Spirit by whom God had spoken in the prophets. He was the Holy Spirit, now descending upon the little band of believers in the risen Lord Jesus Christ. He was the Holy Spirit, who filled the Church with His presence and worked in that Church by His mighty power. And He was the divine Spirit, come from God, given through Christ.

There is one fact written plainly across the pages of the New Testament. It is the fact of an overwhelming, invigorating, unifying reality, which as a great and captivating enthusiasm swept through the primitive Christian band and bound them together in complete dedication to Jesus their risen Lord. In all the variety of experience in the early Christian community, as reflected in this New Testament literature, the unity of spirit is so vivid and real that it can be adequately described only as unity in the Spirit. When we start from these plain facts of human experience, with the confidence, joy, vitality, and fellowship which marked the lives of those who believed in and adored the Lord Jesus, we come to the point where we must move from the realm of the merely human into the realm where we see God the Holy Ghost at work, bearing witness to Jesus as Lord and Saviour and empowering men in their response to this revealing act of God in Christ.

THE CORPORATE LIFE IN THE SPIRIT

Now the central thing in this primitive Christian experience of the presence and power of God the Holy Ghost was that it was not purely individual, but a social and corporate experience. It was the reality of this great enthusiasm which bound the believers together into a community. It was the commanding nature of this great enthusiasm which made it natural for them to say, *It seemed good to the Holy Ghost, and to us . . . (Acts 15:28)*. It was the vigor and refreshment induced by this great enthusiasm that wrought such a remarkable change in the lives of men and women who were baptized into the fellowship of Christian faith.

This fellowship, therefore, was appropriately said by them to manifest *the fellowship of the Holy Ghost*. For it was not their fellowship, created by them out of their own inner spiritual lives as individuals. It was not a community formed because they were united on certain major beliefs or were loyal to some particular ideals. It was a fellowship which they knew had been given to them, into which they felt themselves to be called. It was already established for them to enter. It was God's fellowship. We have spoken of a great enthusiasm. This word means, by derivation, indwelt or possessed by God. For the early Christians, life in the community whose Lord was Jesus Christ was an experience of being possessed by God, and thus it was "life in the Holy Spirit."

It is correct, therefore, to say that while the Holy Spirit is everywhere at work in the world and is to be recognized and adored as God wherever He is seen, that same Holy Spirit is supremely, decisively, and indeed visibly at work in the fellowship of Christians in the Holy Church. The Church, which the New Testament describes as the Body of Christ, is the sphere of the Holy Spirit's intensive presence and operation. It was the Church which at Pentecost received the Holy Spirit.

THE HOLY SPIRIT AND THE CHURCH'S LIFE

EVERYTHING which is rightly done in the Church is done by the power of the Holy Ghost. If this truth is forgotten, and sometimes it has been forgotten, the Church deteriorates into a dull, dead mechanism. When we do not discern or accept the Holy Spirit, the Life-giver, the Church's life turns into a static conventionalism. When, on the other hand, the Holy Spirit is welcomed into His due place of authority, of control, in the life of the Church, that life flowers into a wonderful richness and the Church moves through the world *as an army with banners*.

It is through "the inner witness of the Holy Spirit," as the old writers put it, that we can read the Scriptures with eyes open to see God's mighty hand at work. And it is by the power of the Holy Spirit that the sacraments of the Church are administered by those who are their appointed ministers. The sacraments are not mere rites and ceremonies. The working of the Holy Ghost makes them significant, dynamic, life-giving actions of the Body of Christ. This truth makes absurd and perverse the notion that the Church's sacraments are magic. They are administered by the Church through the operation of the Holy Ghost, who uses them to fill the lives of believers with the life of God and to conform them to the character of the Church's Lord and Head. By sacrament and Scripture, the Christian in the Church becomes like Christ, and through Christ by the Holy Ghost knows the love of God the Father.

Sacrificial living, faithful membership in the Church, prayer and Bible reading, careful and frequent reception of the sacraments, constant opening of the heart and soul and mind to the entrance of the Holy Ghost: this is the Christian life in its fullest sense. But that which is at work in and through the Christian is also to be expressed in all his relationships, in daily life, and common duties. The grace of God, given men by the Holy Ghost, comes to us as a gift. We are able to receive it on one condition. This condition is our readiness to pass on to others what we have been given. The Christian, who is being sanctified by the Spirit, is to be the channel through which that Spirit moves out into the life of the world.

Hence, the Christian Church by its very nature is a missionary society. It is called to spread the gifts of grace. It is to exhibit the love, joy, peace, long-suffering, meekness, temperance, which are *the fruit of the Spirit*. In this way, by demonstrating in life through the Spirit that Gospel which by the same Spirit it proclaims, it is to bring all men to Christ and through Christ to the Father, that *God may be all in all*.

THE WORK OF THE HOLY GHOST

IN the fellowship of the Holy Ghost, men are bound together in a unity which is so strong that none of the usual divisive elements in their experience can pull them apart. In the early days of Christianity the Holy Spirit united men in His fellowship in such a way that St. Paul said, *There is neither Jew nor Greek, there is neither bond nor free, there is neither male nor female (Galatians 3:28)*. All were one in Christ through the Spirit who worked in them. Hence the things that separate men one from another, such as race or culture, social or economic position, sex or class, are overcome in the strength of a unity which holds them together in a common faith, a common love, a common purpose. All men and women, no matter who they are, where they are, what they are, are one in the Spirit as he brings them to Christ in the Church and conforms them to Him, as the Pattern of true manhood in true community.

The work of the Holy Ghost is to *sanctify . . . all the people of God*.[1] Christians know from their experience in the Church that this is the deepest truth about the Holy Ghost. Sanctification is inevitably a social experience. This must be true because the Church is the Body of Christ, a corporate reality and not merely a collection of isolated individual men and women. That will at once suggest another truth, often forgotten these days. To be made "like to Christ" involves, and necessarily must involve, sacrifice. That word and the idea which it suggests are familiar enough in secular affairs. We know what it means to sacrifice for one's country in time of danger. But unhappily, in the Church, we tend to forget the meaning of sacrifice. We often think of Christianity as if it were entirely concerned with helping us to live whole, full, abundant lives, overlooking the equal truth that whole, full, abundant lives are only possible for those who have been radically transformed.

The Holy Spirit does not come to us, therefore, to give

---

[1] Prayer Book, page 285.

us comfort and ease. Indeed, the early Church thought of Him as working almost with violence to wrench men and women out of their easy-going ways into the hard task of following Christ. Jesus Himself told us that sometimes evil eyes had to be plucked out, diseased limbs cut off. *Strait is the gate, and narrow is the way, which leadeth unto life* (*St. Matthew 5:29-30; 7:14*). And while He was Himself sinless, yet He too *learned obedience by the things which he suffered* (*Hebrews 5:8*).

The point is that it is the Holy Spirit in the experience of the Christian who moves him to discipline of soul which involves also discipline of body. This is a part of *the fellowship of Christ's sufferings*. It is part of the very life of the Christian Church and of the life of every individual Christian who is a member of the Church.

THE EXPERIENCE OF THE HOLY SPIRIT

No one of us can ever escape the presence and the power of God the Holy Spirit, sometimes gentle and sometimes overwhelming in His movement through us. But it is only in the Church's fellowship that we may receive the gift of the Holy Spirit and thereby share in a full sense the experience of His supreme action. What is that action? It is so *in*-forming us that we are *con*-formed to Christ, the Lord of Life.

Words change their meaning from age to age. One of the words whose meaning has changed very considerably in the past three centuries is *comfort*. Originally it meant *strength,* as its Latin derivation would suggest. Now it means *ease*. Hence the total misunderstanding of many people when they hear the "Comfortable Words" in the Holy Communion service. They are strengthening words.

Hence, too, the unfortunate idea that the Holy Ghost as the Comforter (which really means the Fortifier or Strengthener) is only our consoler, when in truth He refreshes and vitalizes our lives with the clean current of His energy. To call Him Comforter is to say that He presses, through us and in us and with us, toward God and His revealed will in Jesus, sometimes persuading and sometimes shattering our weak or perverted willing, always working with the vigor and dynamic power of active outgoing love.

In the lives of us all, God the Holy Spirit is at work. In the life of each of us He is at work. These are two sides of one truth: the Holy Spirit working through humanity, socially and individually. He brings men together for great ends, drives the people of the earth into closer community one with another, moves as righteousness and justice among the nations, insists that the order of human society be conformed more closely to the will of God, and shatters our complacent self-interest until we are prepared to coöperate toward this end.

Once again, in that drive within us to answer back in loyalty and love to the Lord Jesus Christ, to be like Him and to serve Him to the best of our ability, we have a clear trace of the Holy Spirit within us. The Holy Spirit is known to us in the pressure of charity in our hearts, impelling us to be helpful, friendly, kindly, brave, honest in all our dealings with our fellow men. He is known to us in that pressure which bids us seek out those who are in need and help them as we can. He is known to us in that pressure which makes us stand firmly for the good thing and the right act and the noble purpose. He is most strikingly known to us as we see ourselves under the judgment of the law implanted in our hearts, and know ourselves as sinners against God.

Finally (and the list is by no means exhausted) in the impulse toward sacrificial living, we have an experience of the Holy Spirit. All that impels us to give up things, to strip ourselves of unnecessary luggage so that we *may run with patience the race that is set before us,* and thus be athletes of God: this is the work of God the Holy Ghost. The discipline which marks the life of the Christian bears its witness to his presence and is made possible by his power.

Here, as we have said, is an element in Christianity which had almost been forgotten. It may be that the sacrifices which are undertaken in time of war, for a secular cause, will help us recover this essential element, will enable our generation to work out a disciplined and integrated pattern of life. It is precisely this which we need more than anything else. We need a pattern or scheme or map or design for our personal life which will give order, dignity, significance, and beauty to what is often a disordered, scattered, chaotic, and meaningless existence. When psychologists talk about integration and a normal life, many of them mean a life adjusted to the social group in which we live. But the more discerning among them see deeper. They know the need of men for adjustment to the reality of God if integrity and normality are to be achieved. But as Christians, we see an even more profound truth. For we know that we can come to lead normal and well-integrated lives only by the power of the Holy Spirit as He molds and shapes our disorganized and inordinate lives, pressing us on toward the pattern of our perfection which is the true man Jesus Christ.

THE DOCTRINE OF THE HOLY GHOST

PRECISELY as with the belief in Christ Himself, so with the Holy Spirit. The facts of experience and the experience of facts forced men to use their minds. As they did so, they came to work out a theology of the Holy Spirit as they had worked out a theology of the person of Christ. This was inevitable. It was also right that they should do so, for our religion is meant to make sense to our minds as well as to warm our hearts and inspire our wills.

What then does the Church teach about the Holy Spirit?

First of all, the Holy Spirit is Lord. This is the affirmation of the Nicene Creed, *And I believe in the Holy Ghost, The Lord. . . .* To call Him Lord means to call Him divine. To call Him divine, if we are Christians, means to call Him God. The English writer, Charles Williams, has spoken of "our Lord God the Holy Spirit." It is a useful phrase, for it reminds us that the divinity of the Holy Spirit is the same as that which we ascribe to Jesus Christ, or to God the Father. The Holy Spirit is true God.

Then, the Holy Spirit is God's power of love binding together the Father and Christ the Son. The particular work of the Spirit, as we might say today, is to be the responsive person in the Triune God.[2] This was shown in the days of our Lord's flesh, for He and the Father were one in love. To the Eternal God there is a response in love. That loving response is divine in origin and nature. The Father is the source of all things, the creator and maker, the unfathomable Reality. The Son is the expressive Person in God, the outgoing Reality who reveals and

---

[2] Once again we approach the doctrine of the Trinity. A fuller presentation of this doctrine will be found in Chapter XII.

manifests the Father. The Holy Spirit is the responding Person in God. He proceeds from the Father through the Son. Through Him, the Son with all that He has manifested and revealed returns to the Father. It is like a circle, returning upon itself. Yet it is not a closed circle, because into it all that has been made by God is taken and brought back to God, perfected and made more and more His own by the action of the Spirit. Of course this is a theological assertion, but it is true to the experience of Christians, as by the Spirit they are conformed to Christ and through Him know God the Father.

Thirdly, the Church always has insisted that the Holy Spirit is not concerned with Church and religion alone. He is *Giver of Life*—of all life. While the New Testament does not contain explicit teaching on the wider aspects of the Spirit's activity, and rightly insists that the gift of the Holy Ghost comes only to those who are members of the Body of Christ, there has been a considerable emphasis, in later theology, on the cosmic work of the Spirit. The Holy Spirit was active in the creation of the world, and He is now active in the natural order. What the biologist, for instance, regards as the drive of nature to conform to some pattern, the Christian theologian regards as the working of the Holy Spirit. It is He who makes the acorn grow up to an oak, the child to manhood, the man to fulfill his potentialities and possibilities. Not that the Holy Spirit *is* life, in the biological sense. That would be pantheism. He is the Spirit in and behind life, the Spirit who makes things grow.

The fourth point is a consequence of this. The Church has said that the Holy Spirit speaks, works, moves, in all sorts of unexpected places. Hence we need never fear new truth since we know that the Holy Spirit is in and behind all truth. As St. Ambrose said, "All truth wherever spoken is spoken by the Holy Ghost." When a famous agnostic writer remarked that somehow he felt that *he* did not produce his books, but that they were produced by "the wind that bloweth through me," we Christians believe that although he failed to realize it, what he felt (if his work was good and true) was the life-giving power of the Holy Spirit. All that was good and true in what he wrote came from that Spirit, whose name he did not know.

When righteousness, goodness, and truth demand assent, we believe the Holy Spirit is there. When the artist van Gogh felt the inward compulsion to paint bright yellow sunlight, a compulsion which was inescapable and to which he was at length bound to yield, we believe that insofar as true beauty was expressed it was by the Holy Spirit working in him. When men are bound together in loyalty to a great and ennobling idea, we believe it is the Holy Spirit at work in them that brings this about. It is our privilege as Christians to recognize in all these areas the manifold and mysterious working of the Spirit *who ordereth all things.*

The scientist seeking truth, the artist expressing beauty, the statesman striving for justice, the soldier giving his life for his comrade, the mother sacrificing for her children, the businessman working honestly for a living, the carpenter at his workbench, the manual laborer digging a ditch—in every department of human life where men seek to live as men, conformed to the truth as they see it, the good as they know it, the right as they believe it—at every point of experience, there is the working of the Holy Spirit.

Often men are seriously misguided in their understanding of the right, the true, the good, and the beautiful. At their best they fail of complete understanding of any of these. Frequently they perversely ignore or even deny what they might know of them. All this we must admit. But we negate our Christian faith if we think to remove God from his world. We are sinners in our thinking if we attempt to confine the activity of the Holy Ghost to the specifically or narrowly religious. It is imperative to say this in order that we may be free from all parochialism, provincialism, and inverted religiosity in our thinking about the Holy Spirit of God.

Yet, while we gladly say this about the wide cosmic work of the Spirit, we have the right and the duty as Christians to insist that we participate in the gift of the Holy Spirit through our membership in the Body of Christ. It is afterward that we can recognize Him at work elsewhere. He speaks, for example, to us in our conscience. Here we need to be careful lest we suggest that any deliverance of the inner voice is necessarily and directly the message of God. Our conscience must be educated, enlightened, trained, and developed by careful, clear thinking about our moral problems. It must be exposed to the best thought that Christians have given to these matters. When this is done, we can be confident that an enlightened conscience is one of the places where the Holy Spirit is known to us, guiding us on our way through life. This leads us to the final and, in a way, the most important point in the Church's teaching about the Holy Spirit.

The Church affirms with sure conviction that the Holy Spirit is the Spirit of the Church, its very life, who guides the Church's deliberations, leads it into all truth, and makes its message ever contemporary. He makes Jesus a present reality, filling men with the grace of Christ as He conforms men to the "image of the Son." He constantly works through the fellowship of the faithful that He may bring the riches of God in Christ into the lives of men wherever they may be. The fruit of the Spirit is released through the Church. Individual lives reflect love, joy, peace, long suffering, meekness, temperance, reverence before God . . . all because God the Holy Ghost, who is Lord and life-giver, indwells the Church and makes it the Church. As men obediently respond by Him and in Him, as He authoritatively takes command of their lives, He binds them into the fellowship of the Holy Ghost.

Thus in our life with God in the Church through sacrament, prayer, and fellowship with our brethren in faith and service to Christ, we have our most direct acquaintance with the Holy Spirit. For there we are in a literal sense living by Him, to the end that we may live in Christ. So it is that in our Christian services of worship we invoke the Holy Spirit. So it is that the *Veni, Creator Spiritus* or some other hymn to the Holy Ghost is sung at ordinations and consecrations. Whenever Christians are gathered together, this is their prayer, unuttered or expressed:

> *Spirit divine, attend our prayers,*
> *And make this house thy home;*
> *Descend with all thy gracious powers,*
> *O come, great Spirit, come!* [3]

Frequently the language of these hymns is a little difficult to modern minds. But that is only because we do not allow the imagination and breadth of thought in religion that we allow elsewhere. Read this great twelfth-century hymn[4] to the Holy Ghost:

---

[3] *The Hymnal 1940,* No. 370.
[4] *The Hymnal 1940,* No. 109.

Come, thou Holy Spirit, come!
And from thy celestial home
  Shed a ray of light divine!
Come, thou Father of the poor!
Come, thou source of all our store!
  Come, within our bosoms shine!

Thou, of comforters the best;
Thou, the soul's most welcome guest;
  Sweet refreshment here below;
In our labor, rest most sweet;
Grateful coolness in the heat;
  Solace in the midst of woe.

O most blessed Light divine,
Shine within these hearts of thine,
  And our inmost being fill!
Where thou art not, man hath naught,
Nothing good in deed or thought,
  Nothing free from taint of ill.

Heal our wounds, our strength renew;
On our dryness pour thy dew;
  Wash the stains of guilt away:
Bend the stubborn heart and will;
Melt the frozen, warm the chill;
  Guide the steps that go astray.

On the faithful, who adore
And confess thee, evermore
  In thy sev'nfold gift descend;
Give them virtue's sure reward;
Give them thy salvation, Lord;
  Give them joys that never end.

Doubtless much of this imagery will seem strange if we are too literal about it. But imagery is meant to be taken with imagination. Coolness, balm, sweet refreshment—here are some of the words used to describe the Holy Ghost. If they do not at once make sense to us, in our experience, let us try turning the phrasing about. Let us say that whenever we know a sense of coolness, refreshment, rest, the Holy Ghost is at work in us. Whenever we have courage in adversity, the Holy Ghost is at work in us. Whenever we love another purely and unselfishly, the Holy Ghost is at work in us. Whenever we adore our Lord and seek to be like Him, the Holy Ghost is at work in us. The tremendous claim of the Christian is that he knows who is at work when these great moments come to him, just as he knows who is at work during the long uneventful periods of *resting in the Lord.*

In response to the question "Where does the sky begin?" the late Bishop Booth of Vermont once said, "In your lungs." Where does the work of God the Holy Ghost begin so far as we have personal and intimate knowledge of Him? In our own lives, when we respond to the best that we know. Supremely, the work of God the Holy Ghost begins when we respond to Jesus Christ in His Body the Church, live by its sacraments, pray its prayers, read its Holy Scriptures, sacrifice ourselves to its Lord, and love the brethren in sincerity.

Then we know that God has given His Spirit and our hearts are made glad *for the operations of his hands.*

The Holy Catholic Church

.

THE Christian faith centers in a Gospel—
a proclamation of the mighty acts of God reaching their
climax in Jesus Christ, in whom God has *visited and redeemed his people*. But the Gospel is not limited to the
spiritual lives of individuals. The Gospel comes to us
through a community of faith, a community reaching
down the years from the days of Jesus when He was with
us in the flesh, yet continuous with the Jewish community
which had preceded it and in which our Lord Himself
made His appearance among men. The result of the coming of Jesus was primarily the establishment of a new
covenant or relationship between God and men, realized
in a new community in which believers appropriated the
Gospel and through which the Gospel came alive for them.
A society was established in which God worked among men
in a new way, yet continued His revelation to His children.
The Church is the new and true Israel, the people of God.
In a word, the Christian Church is integral to the Christian Gospel. There is no such thing as a Christian, in the

historical sense of that word, who is not a member of the Church of God.

When our Lord was withdrawn from the eyes of men, He left with them not a new set of moral principles, not a system of theology, not the inspiration which comes from admiration felt for a great prophet, but He left the Church in which He still lived and through which He continued His work for man's salvation. This is why the Church is included in the Christian Creed. The Nicene Creed puts this in the words, *And I believe one Catholic and Apostolic Church;* the Apostles' Creed says, *I believe in the . . . holy Catholic Church.* The Church is part of the Gospel and Christians throughout the centuries are agreed that there is no saving Gospel which does not include the Church, since the Church is the fellowship in which the Good News is preached, where its meaning is apprehended and realized in the lives of men, and where preëminently men give their witness and support to the Gospel. Here a new relationship (covenant)[1] with God is made possible through the saving grace of Christ.

Now it is quite plain, from all that has been said in the last few chapters, that Christianity involves a creed, something that is believed, not with the mind alone, but with the whole personality. Christianity also involves a life. It makes possible a new quality of experience, provides a new center for loyalty, and engenders a new attitude toward our fellow men.

There is a further truth. Christians throughout the history of the Church have always considered the worship of God their primary duty. Christianity involves not merely a creed and a life, but also a relationship to God known

---

[1] See *The Holy Scriptures* for the idea of covenant.

in Christ through the new covenant which he has established, where, by *the continual remembrance of the sacrifice of the death of Christ,* the Holy Communion, and through the other services of worship, Christian people give God the glory and seek grace for their daily lives. These three elements, belief, life, worship, are intimately related. The Christian Church is the place where we believe, where we worship, and where we find power for living. It is the *blessed company of all faithful people,* because it is the new covenant between God and men in the Body of Christ through which our Lord continually makes Himself known and through which He works in the world of men.

THE CHURCH AS THE BODY OF CHRIST

In many of his letters St. Paul uses the phrase *the body of Christ,* as the most apt description of the Christian fellowship,[2] since the Church bears to our Lord Jesus Christ much the same relationship that our own bodies bear to our innermost selves. It is through our bodies that we express ourselves, that we communicate with other people. No one has ever seen a disembodied person, nor is there normally any communication between spirits without the use of external, bodily means. Of course Christ does not ultimately depend upon His Church, but He has chosen to be with men in a body, a social body. It is a fellowship of believing and adoring men and women, but a body none the less.

Those who belong to Christ are members of His Body. That is why the Catechism and Offices of Instruction in the Prayer Book are so insistent upon the importance of

---

[2] See *The Holy Scriptures,* page 159 ff.

128

Baptism. As the next chapter will show, it is by Baptism that a believer becomes *a member of Christ, the child of God, and an inheritor of the kingdom of heaven.* For our purpose here, the important phrase is *a member of Christ.* We are each and every one of us members in the strict sense. We have toward our Lord the relationship that our arms and legs, our physical members, have toward our physical bodies. We have become, through Baptism, *very members incorporate in the mystical Body* of God the Son, our Saviour and our Lord. We share His life, in order to carry on His work in the power of the Holy Spirit. The Anglican Communion has never forgotten this central fact in its teaching and has never been content to think that a Christian is simply a believer or a disciple. He is that, of course, but he is much more. He is a living part of the living Christ.

Thus the Church is more than a human society for people who happen to share the same ideas or possess the same loyalties. It is a divine creation, brought into being by God Himself when He became incarnate in Christ and died for our sins. It is the new Israel, in which God is fulfilling the promises made to the Jewish people, the old Israel. It is a holy Church, whose secret interior life is the life of Christ Himself, who is the Head of the Body.

It is, of course, true that the members of the Body of Christ are not perfect. We are sinners. We fail to do the will of Christ. We are often in grave error. We are weak and finite beings. But it is even more true to say that in our sin, error, and weakness, we are incorporated into Christ's Church and through the grace which Christ gives in His Church are in process of being made more truly His redeemed people. As men are justified by God's grace through faith, so in the Body of Christ they are also sanctified by grace.

The Church, because the Holy Spirit dwells in it and because it is the Body of Christ, is the community where this sanctification occurs. That which Christ did for us, on Calvary, is now being done in us, as we live faithfully and humbly in His Church, are nourished by His grace through prayer and word and sacrament, and are built up into Him who is our Head. Because this is true, we are called upon to respond to Him, in love and service. The Christian is one who, knowing that Christ died for Him and lives in Him, gives himself in total and grateful allegiance to his Lord.

So it is that the Church is both the mother of the faithful and the proclaimer of the Gospel. It is witness to God's self-manifesting in Christ and it is the community where that revelation, recorded for us in the Bible, most surely touches our lives. It is the sphere where we live in grateful acceptance of that gift. As Christ in His physical body taught the truth about God, brought near the holiness of God, and manifested the reign of God among men, so now in His mystical body He still teaches, sanctifies, and rules among men. We are not perfect, but Christ our Lord is perfect. In His Church, His fullness is given to us and we grow in grace as we seek to know Him, love Him, and serve Him, using the means of grace and looking to the hope of glory.

THE NOTES OF THE CHURCH

The words in our two Creeds, describing the Church, are: *One, Holy, Catholic, Apostolic.* These have often been called the notes of the Church.

The Church is One. This unity is not based upon an external and evident united Christian fellowship existing without division or disagreement. The fact is we are sadly disunited. Yet the Church is one. The unity which we profess in the Creed is already here, in Jesus Christ Himself and in the truth that all who are members of His Body are united in their Lord. It is a unity in Christ. As the Offices of Instruction put it, *the Church is One; because it is one Body under one Head. All baptized persons* are members of the Body, *of which Jesus Christ is the Head.* That is the basic reality upon which we build.

But the changes and chances of history have brought about many divisions among Christian people. Denominations have come into existence, and these have often separated into still other groups. Such division is the consequence of the sinfulness, pride, and stubbornness of men. This does not mean that there were no historical occasions for many of the schisms, or breaches, in the visible unity of the Church. Frequently, the historical justification is plain. These acts of separation were the result of a necessary protest against abuses which, as it appeared, could be corrected in no other way. But whatever the justification, schism is always the reflection of sin. It is sinful. In these days, this is more and more realized. As is shown in *Chapters in Church History,* great movements are afoot to restore the external unity of Christendom. But despite the plainly visible division in that external unity, the Church is at one in its internal and in its eternal reality. It is the Body of Christ. And as Christ cannot be divided, neither can His eternal Church, no matter how broken may be the outward expression of the oneness which we all have in our Lord Jesus Christ. That is why we can sing, *We are not divided, all one Body we. . . .* Our divisions are at a lower level than our great common unity in the Body of Christ. Our present task is to work with vigor, and to pray no less vigorously, for the day when *we may be all of one heart and of one soul, united in one holy bond of truth and peace, of faith and charity, and may with one mind and one mouth glorify*[3] God, through Jesus Christ.

The Church is Holy. Once again, we turn to the Prayer Book Offices of Instruction for guidance on the meaning of this assertion: *The Church is . . . Holy; because the Holy Spirit dwells in it, and sanctifies its members.* When men and women are united together by *the grace of our Lord Jesus Christ,* being assured thereby of *the love of God,* there is realized among them *the fellowship of the Holy Ghost.* This is not just a form of words; it is a real and living truth. The Body of Christ, whose Head is the Lord, is a Holy People, indwelt by the Spirit of the Living God. That Spirit manifests Himself supremely when God's people make their response of faith to the action of God for their redemption.

As a magnet draws to it particles which come within its field, so Christ draws all men to Him. This deep *drawing-to-Christ* is no human affair. It is the sphere of grace, where God's favor, help, and power are known. It is God's own work, and it brings into existence the fellowship whose inner being is the Holy Spirit moving in the world of men. A new relationship has been established with the Holy God. In consequence, the people of God are a holy people in the Holy Church. The Church is the divinely instituted society which has been established by God to make men holy unto Himself.

---

[3] Prayer Book, pages 37-38.

As the Church is knit into a unity by these two actions —God coming to us in Christ, God impelling us to respond in faith to Christ—so its members are sanctified (made holy) by that same Spirit. We have been made members of Christ. We have received the strengthening gift of the Holy Spirit. The result of this gift, as we heard at our own confirmation is *that* [we] *may continue* [God's] *forever; and daily increase in* [the] *Holy Spirit more and more, until* [we] *come unto* [God's] *everlasting kingdom.*[4] There is no magic here. Coöperation of our own wills is essential. We must seek to serve our Lord.

Yet the initiative is with God, not with us, and we pray that as God's fatherly hand is ever with those who are members of Christ's Body, so also His Holy Spirit may *ever be with them; and so lead them in the knowledge and obedience of* [God's] *Word, that in the end they may obtain everlasting life.*

The result of this indwelling and sanctifying work of the Holy Spirit communicated to the faithful in the Church is the manifestation in their own lives, of the *fruit of the Spirit.* St. Paul, as we have seen, describes this in his letter to the Galatians (5:22-23): *love, joy, peace, longsuffering, gentleness, goodness, faith, meekness, temperance.* Increasingly such qualities will be evident in the life of the member of Christ who opens himself to the Spirit and lets Christ, through the Spirit, do His redemptive and sanctifying work.

The Church is Catholic. This word, derived from a Greek word meaning wholeness, has come in English to have an additional meaning. It implies, as the Offices of Instruction say, *universal;* when referred to the Church,

---

[4] Prayer Book, page 297.

it means *holding earnestly the Faith for all time, in all countries, and for all people.* The Body of Christ is the spiritual home of every man who belongs to our Lord, without regard to his race or class, nation or continent. It is his home, whether he lives in the first, the twentieth, or the twenty-fourth century. And the faith which it preaches, as well as the worship which it offers and the life in Christ which it empowers, is for every man, too. That faith, worship, and life are sufficient to bring any man to the full salvation which is offered by God in Christ and witnessed in the Holy Scriptures.

It is, of course, an inevitable consequence of the Church's catholicity that it is a missionary body. Its task is ecumenical, that is, worldwide. It is *sent to preach the Gospel to the whole world.* It is not only a community of those who have themselves already received the saving power given in Christ; it is also a community with a saving mission—to bring the truth of God's redemption to every last man on the earth, so that he may accept the Gospel and be given abundant life in Jesus Christ. It is for this reason that the Christian Church can never be content until the sound of the Gospel is gone out into the ends of the earth. This is why we send evangelists, doctors, teachers, and other missionaries to foreign lands and to the sections of our own country in which the Christian faith has not yet been proclaimed. Christ was sent from God to bring salvation to all men. He is the divine missionary. His Church is His missionary body. In consequence, every member of it is a participant in its missionary labors. In his own town or city, wherever he may be, he, too, is called upon to work for the spread of the Gospel. A Christian who does not realize this demand which the

Gospel lays upon him is by that very token failing in his Christian vocation. Each of us, as a member of the Catholic Church of Christ, has been given a divine commission.

But if *go ye into all the world and make disciples of all nations* (*St. Matthew 28:19*) is part of the meaning of the Church's catholicity, the primary meaning suggested by the word catholic is not to be forgotten. The Church is marked by the quality of wholeness. It is for the whole world. But it also holds the fullness of truth concerning God's saving action in Christ. This is why its faith is called orthodox, or right thinking. Furthermore, its whole life is a unity, in which the faith and worship and Christian action are knit together in an organic fashion. To say this is to say that as in a physical body there is a remarkable inter-relationship of its parts and members, so in the Body of Christ there is an interpenetration of its various aspects. Its belief determines its worship and the character of its ethical teaching. All three make possible its work in the world, and the work of the Church enriches and gives significance to its faith and its approach to God in prayer. Furthermore, every member of the Body is bound up, in one bundle of life, with every other member. We belong to Christ and we belong to one another. *And whether one member suffer, all the members suffer with it; or one member be honored, all the members rejoice with it* (*I Corinthians 12:26*). Here is genuine communion, not only with God in Christ, but also with one another in Him. Such a truth is vitally important, especially in days like our own, when men are lonely, and are seeking a community which will sustain them and give their lives purpose and meaning.

The Church is Apostolic. It *continues stedfastly in the Apostles' teaching and fellowship* (*Acts 2:42*) for its faith

135

is no creation of the present moment but the ancient and everliving commitment to the act of God in Christ, recorded for us in the New Testament, summed up in the Creeds, carried down the centuries in the Christian fellowship, and known in worship and work by centuries of believing men and women. We are members of a vast company, whom no man can number, who have lived in the faith, shared in the life, and found strength in the worship. The origin of these things is told us in the Bible and their continuing vitality is demonstrated daily as we play our proper part in the Church's company.

The Church's apostolicity is the guarantee that we are united with the apostles themselves, the earliest witnesses to God's redemption in Christ. When we take our place in the Church we accept as our own *the faith once delivered to the saints (Jude 1:3)*, rather than some particular theory or speculation as to the meaning of Christianity. But this does not mean that the task of rethinking the historic faith is unnecessary. On the contrary, the very fact that we are given the faith out of the rich experience of the past demands that we do our best to express it in a way so vivid and so full of meaning that the contemporary world will see its truth, its relevance, and its necessity. On the other hand, the apostolicity of the Church makes it plain that we are never to substitute for the Gospel some other or easier way of life. *This is the way, walk ye in it.*

The Church which is the Body of Christ is set in the world to conform the world to God's will as He has made it known in Christ. The implications of this are clear. The Church is to be conformed to Christ, not to the world. If it does not conform itself to our Lord, it denies its essential nature. Its faith is not just the common belief of good men.

It is the faith in God's act for all men. Its Gospel is both the fulfillment of whatever good may be discovered anywhere, and the sharp condemnation of all that is evil wherever that may be found. *The word of God . . . is sharper than a twoedged sword (Hebrews 4:12)*; and there come times when that sword must cut to the very marrow so that unrighteousness and injustice may be destroyed. This is part of the prophetic task of the Church.

THE CHURCH'S PRIESTLY NATURE

ON the other hand, the Church has a priestly task. Its joy is to offer the creation, including the human creation, to God in perfect surrender. In the Holy Communion this is done in a specific and sacramental fashion.[5] But the same offering is the task of the Church in every aspect of its work—to take the things of the world and dedicate them to God's service, so that His will may be done and His kingdom come, on earth as it is in heaven. All members of the Church are involved in this priestly vocation. We need only recall the New Testament description of Christians as *a chosen generation, a royal priesthood, an holy nation, a peculiar people (I Peter 2:9)*. Of course, there is only one High Priest, our Lord Jesus Christ. But those who are members of His Body are each and every one a sharer, by His grace, in that priesthood which is His and which marks His Church precisely because it is His body. This is the scriptural meaning of "the priesthood of all believers." It is misleading to say that this means today, as in early times in Israel, that "every man is his own priest before God." It means, rather, that all who belong to Christ's holy people are by grace sharers in Christ's priesthood. By sharing in

---

[5] See Chapter X.

that priesthood they have direct access through Him to God. This has its important corollary in the fact that every Christian is therefore also priest to God for his brethren, because he shares Christ's high priesthood.

It is against this background that we must understand the ordained ministry since its particular task in the Body of Christ is to represent and function for the whole Body in its several responsibilities. A deacon, priest, or bishop is not separated from the Church or its lay members by some impassable gulf. He is the agent of Christ, in His Church, to perform those special functions which are necessary both for the continuation of the Church's life and the fulfillment of what is the task of the whole fellowship. A bishop, for example, is *to be a chief pastor in the Church; to confer Holy Orders; and to administer Confirmation.*[6] A priest is *to minister to the people committed to his care; to preach the Word of God; to baptize; to celebrate the Holy Communion; and to pronounce Absolution and Blessing in God's Name.* A deacon is *to assist the Priest in Divine Service, and in his other ministrations.* These definitions of function, found in the Offices of Instruction, make clear the way in which those ordained to the ministry of the Church are to act as *Messengers, Watchmen, and Stewards of the Lord.* God, we believe, has appointed by His Holy Spirit *divers Orders of ministers*[7] in His Church. They are so appointed, as St. Paul reminds us, not to lord it over our faith, but to be helpers of our joy.[8]

This ministry, the Ordinal tells us, is *from the Apostles' time.* The *Ministers of Apostolic Succession,* in the Prayer Book phrase (page 572), are believed by Anglicans

---

[6] For this whole series of definitions, see Prayer Book, page 294.
[7] Prayer Book, pages 531, 537; also 39.
[8] II Corinthians 1:24.

138

to maintain our continuity with the ancient Church and to symbolize in a living ministry the apostolic character of the Holy Church of Christ. In this sense, the bishop, who is the chief pastor in the Church, stands for and symbolizes the deep reality of the Church as sent by God in Christ to preach the Gospel, administer the sacraments, shepherd the flock, and bring all things into captivity to our Lord. Those whom he ordains are given authorization to minister for Christ in His Church; and their ministry is thus authenticated as being the ministry which comes to us from the time of the apostles. In order to make certain that a ministry of this character is continued, our Church has required that *no man shall be accounted or taken to be a lawful Bishop, Priest, or Deacon, in this Church, or suffered to execute any of the said Functions, except he be called, tried, examined, and admitted thereunto. . . .*[9] It requires that such admittance to the ministry shall be by *Episcopal Consecration or Ordination.*

Our communion gladly recognizes God's blessing upon other ministries which have not been episcopally transmitted. But Anglicanism maintains the ancient ministry and treasures it as a witness to the organic continuity of the Church. In official statements our communion has held that

1. The historical episcopate
2. The unfailing appeal to Holy Scripture
3. The use of the Nicene and the Apostles' Creeds, and
4. The two Gospel sacraments of Baptism and Holy Communion

are central elements in the Christian tradition as we have received it and as we teach it. The Chicago-Lambeth Quad-

---

[9] Preface to Ordinal, Prayer Book, page 529.

rilateral,[10] whose four points we have thus briefly summarized, has stated the general requisites, which, consistent with the Anglican Church's loyalty to its whole heritage, can be used as the basis for discussions with other groups of Christians concerning the reunion of Christendom.

In sum, the fact that the Church is declared in our Creeds to be One, Holy, Catholic, and Apostolic means that the Christian tradition is an integral and unified reality, grounded in the historical events to which the Scriptures bear witness, nourished by the devotion of saints and humble men of heart, conveyed to us through the means of grace, and shared in fellowship with our brethren, living and dead. The vitality and the validity or truth of Christianity are closely related. This is the living community of faith we call the COMMUNION OF SAINTS.

---

[10] This Quadrilateral, adopted at Lambeth in 1888 by the archbishops and bishops of the Anglican Communion, was based on a similar document prepared in the American Church. This was approved by General Convention in Chicago in 1886. It sets forth the position of our communion on matters of Christian reunion. Compare *Chapters in Church History*, pages 252 ff.

The Communion of Saints and the Forgiveness of Sins

THE Christian Church is the communion of saints, the blessed company of all faithful people. Some of this great company are now living and constitute the Church militant here on earth. But there are those, including the vast proportion of Christians, who have died in faith and now rest from their labors. They make up what has often been called the Church Expectant and the Church Triumphant. Some of them have been great saints, whose loyalty to Christ, even to the point of death, has been recognized by sure instinct, so that they are mentioned by name in the Church's Calendar. They are saints; but so are all who have been redeemed and made partakers of the risen life of Christ. The New Testament is very clear about this: St. Paul tells us, for example, that we are all saints, *i.e.,* holy people, if we belong to Christ and *daily increase in* [the] *Holy Spirit.*

We sing in a familiar hymn of *all the saints who from their labors rest.* Many of them we can mention by name, recalling with a glad mind their devout lives, their brave confession of the name of Christ, their humble service of their Lord. They set before us a rich variety of examples of Christian life, showing us many different refractions of Christ who is the Light of the World. Others, whose names we do not know, we commemorate each year on All Saints' Day, when we give God *high praise and hearty thanks for the wonderful grace and virtue which he has declared* in them. Those who have departed from this life, but who we cannot say are already made perfect, are yet like us, saints in the making. They have been signed with the Cross in Baptism and are therefore members of Christ's Body. Thus the Church prays for them, that they may have *continual growth in* [God's] *love and service.*[1] We ask that they may *go from strength to strength, in the life of perfect service.*[2] We unite our own attempt to live the life in Christ, with their example of that life, and we ask that we too may have the grace which was given them, so that we may all be partakers of God's heavenly kingdom.

This communion of saints in which we are in fellowship with all our companions in the faith of Christ crucified is especially real to us in the Holy Communion, when *with Angels and Archangels, and all the company of heaven,* we laud and magnify God's holy name. We present before our heavenly Father the sacrifice which His only-begotten Son accomplished for our redemption, so that we may be filled with His grace and heavenly benediction. In performing this action, we are united with the whole company of the

---

[1] Prayer Book, page 75.
[2] Prayer Book, page 332.

saints, who like us are made one body with Christ that He may dwell in us and we in Him. Death, for those who live by such a faith, is no barrier to fellowship in Christ with those whom we have loved in Him.

Fellowship means common concern. And just as we continue to pray for those we love when they have died, so we believe that those in the nearer presence of God hold before God our needs and concerns in intercessory prayer. We believe that in our every effort here for God's cause we are encompassed by a great cloud of witnesses. The fullest implications of our faith in the communion of saints are drawn out in a beautiful collect in the Scottish Book of Common Prayer:

O God the King of saints, we praise and magnify thy holy Name for all thy servants who have finished their course in thy faith and fear; for the Blessed Virgin Mary, for the holy Patriarchs, Prophets, Apostles and Martyrs, and for all thy other righteous servants; and we beseech thee that, encouraged by their example, strengthened by their fellowship, and aided by their prayers, we may attain unto everlasting life; through the merits of thy Son Jesus Christ our Lord. Amen.

To be a Christian means to be a member of the Body of Christ, accepting its faith in the Bible's gospel proclamation of God's redeeming work in Christ. It means living the life which St. Paul described as being *in Christ,* nourished and strengthened by the sacraments which *Christ hath ordained in his Church.* The sacraments and the preaching of the Word, both exhibiting God's revelation and both rooted in the Holy Scriptures, which are the record and witness of God's revelation, are the Church's means of grace.

But what is grace? It is the help of God, His favor toward us, and His power given to us, so that we may fulfill His will and live acceptably before Him. It is a personal reality, not a force. Like the love of a friend, it creates a new relationship. In fact, grace is God's love in action. As means of grace, therefore, the sacraments of the Church are essential and a primary way in which our Lord, who is Head of the Church, carries on this sanctifying work in us who are His members, so that we may realize our membership in the communion of saints, be nourished by the life of Christ, and be restored to the fullness of our membership when we have sinned. Thus we may be more and more perfectly united with Christ and empowered to live as His holy people in this world of time and space.

WHY SACRAMENTS?

FIRST of all, we must try to understand why it is that Holy Baptism, Holy Communion, and the other rites of a sacramental nature should have their part and place in the Christian scheme of things. For to some it may seem that such sacramental ways of approach to God are not as spiritual as Christ's religion might appear to be. What is the reason for sacraments and for a sacramental way of worship?

The answer to this question may be approached by a brief consideration of the nature of man himself. As was pointed out in earlier chapters, man is by no means a purely spiritual creature. He is not adequately described when we speak of him as a living soul; after all, he has a body. Every one of us is a strange combination of soul and body. We might perhaps say that man is a soul-body organism. Psychosomatic medicine, recognizing the intimate relation of mind and body, emphasizes this today. The fact also is demonstrated in all our human behavior. We see through our eyes, we hear with our ears, we understand with our physical brains, we walk on our feet, and we talk with our mouths. In every instance, we are necessarily using some bodily means to communicate our ideas, to express our thoughts, to speak of our concern or love, to get from one place to another. Otherwise, we should not be able to do anything at all.

Furthermore, our ability to receive ideas and impressions, our acceptance of that which those outside us wish to convey to us, is made possible by a physical or bodily medium. Things which are in our minds come to us through the bodily senses with which we are endowed. Indeed, it is in this way that we really live as men. As someone has said, we are amphibians, living as spirits in bodies, or as minds with bodies. We learn what we learn and do what we do through the instrumentality of these bodies.

The world in which we live is constructed on the same principle. We speak of love and beauty and truth. But no one has ever seen love or beauty or truth. When we speak of love, for example, we mean that we have seen actions which are loving. When we speak of beauty, we are saying that we have observed things that are beautiful. When we speak of truth, we are asserting that we have heard statements which are true.

When we say that a purpose is being worked out in the world, we are not pretending that we can actually see the purpose itself; we mean that we see the various activities and the many events which are the instruments through which the purpose is worked out. From that observation we come to understand something of what is being done and so discern the purpose which is being demonstrated.

Yet we all say we know these things. There is a spirit or mind or soul which uses the body, the physical realities, material objects, times and places, as its way of establishing relationships with that which is outside it.

THE INCARNATION AND THE SACRAMENTAL PRINCIPLE

Now all this is closely related to the great Christian affirmation that God became man in Jesus Christ our Lord.[3] St. John's Gospel tells us that *the Word was made flesh* (*St. John 1:14*). This is a clear statement that when God, our Creator, wished to make Himself known to men in the most compelling manner possible He employed for His purpose the human life which was born of the Virgin Mary. He created, by His Holy Spirit, our Lord's human life. Having created it, He remained with it and in it, in personal union, so that it was not just a human life, but always and to eternity God's human life. But see what this implies. It means that God uses bodily, physical, and human means of communication with men, that He accomplishes our salvation through a material human body hanging on a material cross,[4] that He accommodates Himself to the very terms upon which we, precisely because we are men, must necessarily live. That is what it means to talk about the Incarnation, the en-*flesh*-ment and en-*man*-ment of Almighty God himself.

The Prayer Book Catechism (page 581) has a brief and telling definition of a sacrament. It says that a sacrament is *an outward and visible sign of an inward and spiritual*

[3] See Chapter VI.
[4] Strictly speaking, through the total humanity of Jesus, body and soul. But in this context we are speaking particularly of the way in which God uses the physical and material, as well as the spiritual, to communicate with men.

146

grace given unto us; ordained by Christ himself, as a means whereby we receive the same, and a pledge to assure us thereof. Surely Jesus Christ is the supreme sacrament. For here the outward and visible, a human life in all its richness, is the means by which *an inward and spiritual* reality, God Himself, is given to us and known by us. God is not too spiritual to use material things; He deliberately chooses to employ them, and by doing so He has consecrated to Himself physical realities such as we all know in our daily experience. God makes Himself known to us through the things that are.

It is for this reason that the Christian Church in its corporate life has found that the sacramental way of response to God is the fulfillment of all other ways. Because this sacramental way ministers to the whole of man's structure and experience, it has proved to be the normal and most satisfying means of grace. After all, God Himself approaches us in a sacramental fashion in Christ. It is very dangerous to try to be more spiritual in our response to God than He is in His approach to us. We now turn to examine briefly each of the Church's sacraments or sacramental ordinances.

Although there has been a reference in this chapter to the Sacrament of the Lord's Supper or Holy Communion, we shall start this more detailed discussion with a consideration of Holy Baptism. The Holy Communion is clearly the constant sacrament in Christian experience; but it is through the Sacrament of Holy Baptism that we become Christians. That is why it must have the first place. Both of these sacraments were ordained by Christ as a means whereby we receive grace and as a pledge to assure us of that fact. The Holy Scriptures record for us their institution by our Lord. They were given to us by Him as *certain sure witnesses, and effectual signs of grace, and God's good will toward us, by the which he doth work invisibly in us, and doth not only quicken, but also strengthen and confirm our Faith in him.*[5]

BAPTISM

EVERY society or organization has some rite of initiation by which those who would become members are brought into the group and given the rights and privileges which will belong to them as members. So it is that the Christian Church has its initiation into membership. But this Christian rite is very different from initiation into some merely human society. It also is entrance into the mystical Body of Christ, where His redemption is known and His grace is given. The Prayer Book (page 292) tells us what this means, *The inward and spiritual grace in Baptism is a death unto sin, and a new birth unto righteousness; whereby we are made the children of grace.* Water is poured on the candidate (or he may be immersed, if he so desire), as these words are said, *I baptize thee In the Name of the Father, and of the Son, and of the Holy Ghost. Amen.* With this outward and visible sign, the candidate for baptism becomes *a member of Christ, the child of God, and an inheritor of the kingdom of heaven.* He receives a name, a *Christian* name, as a token that hereafter he is not only one among many members of the human race, but is also, and to all eternity, God's child, known by name.[6]

The new Christian is received *into the congregation of Christ's flock . . . grafted into the body of Christ's*

---

[5] Articles of Religion, Article XXV.

[6] See the whole Office of Holy Baptism, Prayer Book, pages 273 ff, for most of the quotations in this section.

Church. This means that new resources are available to him. He shares in the life of the whole Body, and more and more he is conformed to the character of the Church's Lord. Baptism makes available to him the treasures of Christ. But the degree to which he enters into this heritage will depend upon his response, the example of other Christians, and the measure in which Christian faith and life are actually manifested in that part of the visible Church with which he is in touch. Because there is no limit to what God wills for the person and because of the fullness of that into which he can grow, our baptismal service says that he is *regenerate,* that is, *born again* into a new family. He enters into its way of life. He is already made over, in principle and by anticipation. Thus there are made available for him the fruits of Christ's victory over sin and death, once-for-all accomplished on Calvary. That is why the effects of baptism are described as remission of sin and participation in the Resurrection life.

Of course the baptism of an adult represents a conscious change in his commitments. He has repented of his sins and has come to faith in the promises of God. But the person to be baptized may be an infant, who cannot possess these things. It is then that the love of God comes to him, long before he can respond to it. By God's prevenient grace, as the Church says, he is taken into Christ's Body. Through the faith of the whole Church the infant is supplied with that which he himself cannot supply. Especially through the living personal faith of his parents and sponsors, the Church provides this for him. Thus from earliest years the child can *become the recipient of* [God's] *grace, and be trained in the household of faith.*[7] And because, adult or

---

[7] Prayer Book, page 292.

child, he is by baptism made one of God's faithful children, the new Christian is expected *to confess the faith of Christ crucified, and manfully to fight under his banner, against sin, the world, and the devil; and to continue Christ's faithful soldier and servant unto his life's end.* The presence of sponsors or witnesses and their promises, assures the newly baptized person of the help of his fellow Christians in his endeavor to serve Christ in his Church.

It is at Baptism that we become members of the Church. But it is at Confirmation that the initiation into our membership is completed. In the primitive Church when those baptized were for the most part adults these two rites were administered together, as they still are even for children in the Eastern Church. As the years went on, however, and the custom of infant baptism was more generally practiced, the Western Church deemed it wiser to wait until years of discretion had been reached before the young Christian should be granted full entrance into all the privileges of Christian participation, chiefly admission to the Holy Communion. But the earlier custom (still followed by Eastern Orthodox Christians) indicates that Baptism and Confirmation are not two separate rites; rather, Confirmation is the complement and completion of our Baptism.

THE LORD'S SUPPER OR HOLY COMMUNION

THE Sacrament of the Lord's Supper or Holy Communion has a special place in our Christian life and worship. The Prayer Book (page 86) tells us, in one of the exhortations printed at the end of the Order of Holy Communion, that Christ *hath instituted and ordained holy mysteries, as pledges of his love, and for a continual remembrance of his death, to our great and endless comfort.* And in the exhortation immediately following (pages 87), we are told that *Almightly God, our heavenly Father, hath given his Son our Saviour Jesus Christ, not only to die for us, but also to be our spiritual food and sustenance in that Holy Sacrament.* This great service, which one of the collects (page 294) calls *the blessed Sacrament of the Body and Blood of Christ,* has ever been the focus of Christian devotion. It may be called the most holy of all the holy things with which God has endowed His Church.

This great Christian act of worship has been celebrated under many different names by the Christian Church since that night when our Lord took bread and blessed it, and giving it to His disciples, said *This is my Body.*[8] Whether it is known as the Lord's Supper, Holy Communion, or Holy Eucharist,[9] whether it is called the Mass, as in the Roman Catholic Church, in certain Lutheran Churches, and in the First English Prayer Book of 1549, or whether it is described as the Divine Liturgy as in the Eastern Orthodox Church, it is the same service. In the words of the Catechism, it was ordained for *the continual remembrance of the sacrifice of the death of Christ, and of the benefits which we receive thereby.*[10]

In this sacrament "the whole meaning of our salvation is comprehended." Those are words first written by St. Thomas Aquinas, and the English Reformers echo his thought, for they speak[11] of *the most comfortable Sacrament of the Body and Blood of Christ; to be by* [Christians] *re-*

----

[8] The accounts of the institution of Holy Communion are found in St. Matthew 26:26-29; St. Mark 14:22-25; St. Luke 22:14-20; and in I Corinthians 11:23-26.

[9] The Prayer Book uses the term *Holy Eucharist* in the Office of Institution of Ministers.

[10] Prayer Book, page 293.

[11] Prayer Book, page 86.

ceived in remembrance of his meritorious Cross and Passion; whereby alone we obtain remission of our sins, and are made partakers of the Kingdom of heaven. Here, as the Prayer of Consecration says, we *do celebrate and make . . . before* [God's] *Divine Majesty, with these* [his] *holy gifts,* which we here offer to him, the memorial Christ commanded us to make, *having in remembrance his blessed passion and precious death, his mighty resurrection and glorious ascension; rendering unto* [God] *most hearty thanks for the innumerable benefits procured unto us by the same.*[12]

Men who have glimpsed, if for a moment, the unutterable holiness and majesty of the living God; men who have known, if for a moment, the depths of their own sinfulness, weakness, and shame; men who have understood, if for a moment, their terrible need of redemption—men, everywhere and at every time, have sought to offer to God something which would in some way atone for their sin and reconcile them to God. In a way, that is the story of the human race: the search for some offering which will be acceptable to God. But this is a futile search. Man cannot find an offering acceptable to God. But that which man could not find God Himself has provided. What is it? It is human life, a human life, the true human life poured out in death, given in perfect love and obedience to God. It is the Lord Jesus, *the Lamb of God that taketh away the sins of the world.*

The Church, therefore, offers to God the memorial which *Christ commanded.* By His death on Calvary, He made the *one full, perfect, and sufficient sacrifice, oblation, and satisfaction, for the sins of the whole world.*[13] The Church, on

---

[12] Prayer Book, pages 80-81.
[13] Prayer Book, page 80.

its part, in the Eucharist offers *this our sacrifice of praise and thanksgiving*.[14] It is an action, something which is done, following our Lord's command, *Do this in remembrance of me*. The Christian way of remembering our Lord's redeeming work is not only by thinking about it or turning back to it in mind, but also by repeating an action—taking, breaking, blessing, giving, as Christ did at the Last Supper in the Upper Room in *the night in which he was betrayed*. This action is set in the context of a great thanksgiving to God for His redemption of men through His Incarnate Son. Hence the word Eucharist, which is Greek for thanksgiving. The Holy Communion is not a sad service. It is a joyous gathering of Christians to *celebrate*.[15] The words in the Holy Communion in the 1549 Prayer Book appropriately describe the atmosphere of the service: *Let us make a joyful feast unto the Lord*.

The Eucharist, therefore, is the divinely appointed way in which the Christian Church makes its *continual remembrance of the sacrifice of the death of Christ*.[16] But as we have seen, the *remembrance* is not just a turning-back in pious reverie to the days of Christ's life and passion and resurrection. It is a living remembrance in which He comes to us with all His redemptive power. That means that He is Himself present as the Eucharist is celebrated. The manner in which Christ is present and communicates Himself to His people in the Holy Communion has never been precisely defined by the Anglican Churches, although the certainty and reality of His presence have been strongly affirmed. Anglicanism accepts Christ's promise that the

---

[14] Prayer Book, page 81.
[15] See Hymn 206 in *Hymnal 1940* for a beautiful statement of this theme.
[16] Prayer Book, page 293.

communicant is made a sharer in the very life of Christ Himself present in the Eucharist. By receiving Christ in the sacramental action, he is enabled to live in Christ as Christ lives in him. The Prayer Book tells us that *the inward part, or thing signified* by the *Bread and Wine, which the Lord hath commanded to be received,* is *the Body and Blood of Christ, which are spiritually taken and received by the faithful in the Lord's Supper.*[16] In consequence of this, those who are partakers in the Lord's Supper receive through Holy Communion the strengthening and refreshing of their souls by *the Body and Blood of Christ, as their bodies are strengthened and refreshed by the Bread and Wine.*[16]

> *And now, O Father, mindful of the love*
> *That bought us, once for all, on Calvary's tree,*
> *And having with us him that pleads above,*
> *We here present, we here spread forth to thee,*
> *That only off'ring perfect in thine eyes,*
> *The one true, pure, immortal sacrifice.*
>
> *Look, Father, look on his anointed face,*
> *And only look on us as found in him;*
> *Look not on our misusings of thy grace,*
> *Our prayer so languid, and our faith so dim;*
> *For lo! between our sins and their reward,*
> *We set the passion of thy Son our Lord.*[17]

In thus spreading forth Christ's "one true, pure, immortal sacrifice," the Body of Christ which is the Church offers itself to the Father, in union with its Head: *And here we offer and present unto thee, O Lord, ourselves,*

---

[16] Prayer Book, page 293.
[17] *Hymnal 1940,* No. 189.

154

*our souls and bodies, to be a reasonable, holy, and living
sacrifice unto thee.*[18] At the same time that it is offering
itself, in and through its members, it is also offering back
to God the life of the whole human race, and indeed the
entire creation, praying that through Christ all things may
be made holy and serviceable to the God who created them
and has redeemed them to Himself by the Sacrifice on Calvary.

St. Augustine wrote[19] some profound words on this subject when he told his people that they were to offer the
mystery of their own lives to God as they presented before
their heavenly Father the sacrificial memorial of the Passion of Christ. When they did this, he said, they would receive back from God, in a mystery, that which they had
offered to Him. So it is that the Church, which is Christ's
mystical Body, offers itself in union with the sacrifice of
Christ on Calvary, to the end that its members may receive
Christ's Body and Blood and be empowered to become
more fully that which by His redemption they are. This
may be a difficult saying; certainly it demands most careful
thought and meditation. Yet it touches the essence of Christianity. It means that those who are members of Christ's
Church and are nourished by Christ's life through the sacrament are to live as befits Christ's Body. The continual
remembrance of Christ's sacrifice, and communion in the
Body and Blood of Christ, lead directly to action for Christ.
We are to do by God's grace *all such good works as* [he]
hast prepared for us to walk in.[20]

*   *   *

[18] Prayer Book, page 81.
[19] Both in his sermons and in *The City of God.*
[20] Prayer Book, page 83.

WE now turn to other Prayer Book rites which are of a sacramental character in that they involve both an outward and visible sign, and an inward and spiritual grace. These rites are Confirmation, Absolution, Holy Orders, Matrimony, and Anointing or Unction. Provision is made for each of them in the Prayer Book.

CONFIRMATION

WE already have mentioned confirmation in the discussion of the nature of the Church of Christ and of baptism. Here we must be content with a brief summary of the theology of the Prayer Book service which makes clear the meaning of the action. Confirmation is performed by the bishop, who by the outward and visible sign of the Laying on of Hands, with the use of prayer, calls down upon the candidates the Holy Spirit of God to strengthen them in their Christian profession. By this action they receive *the wisdom and understanding, the counsel and ghostly strength, the knowledge, true godliness and holy fear,*[21] which are the Spirit's gifts to the members of Christ's Church.

These gifts are not the virtues which we call by such names, so much as they are the capacities to act virtuously, by God's power and help, so that the Christian may increasingly manifest the fruit of the Spirit whose gifts have already been given him.

As a preparation for this strengthening by the Holy Spirit, the one to be confirmed renews the solemn promise and vow that he made when baptized, or that his sponsors in baptism made for him, and undertakes in a responsible way the life of a Christian disciple. Having made this

---

[21] Prayer Book, page 297.

pledge, he is confirmed. Note that the Prayer Book[22] tells us that the person *is* confirmed. The primary action is the work of God the Holy Ghost, through the bishop. It is not simply a human ratification or confirmation of promises already made, although it is also that. God is at work here; man responds, but God first acts. The work of Baptism is completed and initiation into Christian membership is brought to its fullness.

ABSOLUTION

THE Prayer Book includes among the functions of a priest the duty of pronouncing *Absolution . . . in God's Name;*[23] and states that God *hath given power, and commandment, to his Ministers, to declare and pronounce to his people, being penitent, the Absolution and Remission of their sins.*[24] One way in which this ministry is exercised is through corporate confession in public worship. In this corporate or general confession of sins, the participants in worship affirm their sinfulness, their desire for forgiveness and their intention to lead a new life, *walking from henceforth in God's holy ways.* Such confession should always involve a genuine acknowledgment of actual sins as well as a more general statement of one's sinfulness. It is because of the sincerity of confession by those present at the public services of the Church that the priest's declaration of forgiveness is effectual.

This priestly declaration and pronouncement given in public worship, however, is not all that our Church provides for sinning men and women who are troubled in

---

[22] Page 295, the third rubric after the Offices of Instruction.
[23] Offices of Instruction, Prayer Book, page 294.
[24] Morning Prayer, Prayer Book, page 7.

conscience by their failure to do God's will. In the exhortation printed at the end of the Order of Holy Communion (page 88) the priest is directed to say: *If there be any of you, who . . . cannot quiet his own conscience . . . but requireth further comfort or counsel, let him come to me or to some other Minister of God's Word, and open his grief; that he may receive such godly counsel and advice, as may tend to the quieting of his conscience, and the removing of all scruple and doubtfulness.* And in the Visitation of the Sick (page 313) we read: *Then shall the sick person be moved to make a special confession of his sins, if he feel his conscience troubled with any matter; after which confession, on evidence of his repentance, the Minister shall assure him of God's mercy and forgiveness.*

Many Christians, including those who are in good physical health, have found it helpful to make a private and specific acknowledgment of their sins to God through sacramental confession in the presence of a priest of the Church. When they do this, they can receive from him both absolution from sin and assurance that they are restored by God to living membership in Christ's Body. No member of the Church is required to seek this help; its use is voluntary and not a matter of imposed obligation. But the Prayer Book encourages it for those who are troubled in conscience, and others have found it a way to quicken the conscience and to grow in grace. Through its use many have discovered the *joy and peace in believing* which should mark every Christian man, woman, and child. It is indeed a privilege of which many avail themselves as a means of continuing as *Christ's faithful soldiers and servants.*

THE purpose of Holy Matrimony is *to join together this Man and this Woman*,[25] so that in that *honorable estate, instituted of God, signifying unto us the mystical union that is betwixt Christ and his Church,* they may *live together in faithfulness and patience, in wisdom and true godliness,* with their home *a haven of blessing and of peace.* It is appropriate, therefore, that the Church should bless a marriage, so that the two who are to become husband and wife *may surely perform and keep the vow and covenant betwixt them made.*

The ministers of Holy Matrimony are the couple who are undertaking the marriage; by their promises they marry themselves, each to the other. But the priest, acting as the representative of the Church, *solemnizes the marriage* by pronouncing upon the union blessing in God's name. As a consequence of this union blessed by the Church on God's behalf, the man and woman are given the grace which our heavenly Father bestows upon all who share in His work in creating. For marriage is not only an outward and visible sign of the inward and spiritual love between the two, but is also God's appointed method of continuing the human race. Yet, with that gift there comes new responsibility. For Christians who are members of the Church of Christ, marriage is not merely a means of legalizing sexual relations; it is sacramental in nature, permanent in character, and must reflect the *spiritual marriage and unity* that exists between the Lord and His Church which, as the Prayer Book tells us, is His *Bride and Spouse.* This is the reason that the Anglican Church, in all its branches both in America and

---

[25] See the Marriage Office, Prayer Book, pages 300-304, for the quotations in this section.

abroad, places such weight upon the vow of lifelong union of man and wife *till death us do part.*

HOLY ORDERS

THE ordained ministry of the Church of Christ is marked, says the Ordinal (Prayer Book, page 539), by both dignity and great importance. The clergy are not only members of the Church commissioned by their fellow Churchmen to preach and take services; they are expected to be called of God and are set apart to represent Christ in His Church. Hence the act of ordination has a sacramental character.

In our Church, the bishop is the minister of ordination. He lays his hands upon those who are called to the diaconate. With other priests, he lays hands on those to be ordained to the priesthood. With other bishops, he lays hands upon those who are to be consecrated to the episcopate. The words which are used at this imposition of hands indicate that by this action, accompanied with prayer, God the Holy Ghost sets apart and authenticates these persons as ministers of Christ in His Church.

Earlier in this book we have discussed the particular functions which the deacon, the priest, and the bishop may exercise. They perform these functions, not as if they were ministering from outside to the Church, but as those who within the Church act for it in the name of Christ. They are ministers of God's Holy Word and they are dispensers of God's Holy Sacraments, performing these offices within the context of the whole Church of Christ, whose representatives they are. In that they are representatives of the whole Church of Christ, they are by that very token and by Christ's action through the Holy Spirit designated His ministers, to and for His people.

THE MINISTRY OF HEALING AND
UNCTION OF THE SICK

In *St. James's Epistle* (5:14-15) we read that in the first days of Christianity, when one was sick he called for *the elders of the Church,* who *prayed over him, anointing him with oil in the name of the Lord.* This *prayer of faith,* it is said, *shall save the sick and the Lord shall raise him up.* The practice of anointing those in sickness has continued to be a Christian rite down through the centuries. In the medieval Church it unfortunately became limited to those at the point of death. But it is in keeping with the earlier Christian practice that the Prayer Book (page 320) provides a form to be used when it is desired by any who are ill.

The sacramental nature of this action is shown in the direction that the minister may use a prayer in which he says, *I anoint thee with oil* (or *I lay my hand upon thee*), *In the Name of the Father, and of the Son, and of the Holy Ghost, beseeching the mercy of our Lord Jesus Christ, that all thy pain and sickness of body being put to flight, the blessing of health may be restored unto thee.* Coupled with this prayer is another, in which God is asked not only to *drive away all pain of soul and body,* but also *to release thy servant from sin.* Here an outward and visible means is being employed so that an inward and spiritual gift may be received.

Now that we are becoming more conscious of the psychosomatic nature of much illness, it is particularly significant that we should find embedded in the tradition and practice of Christ's Church a means of grace whose object is to assist in the restoration of wholeness of body as well as of soul. It is probably for this reason that there is an increasing emphasis throughout the Episcopal Church upon

the healing ministry, which endeavors to bring the resources of the Gospel along with the best medical and psychiatric skill to those who are afflicted in body or mind.

THE SACRAMENTAL WAY AND HUMAN LIFE

IT is remarkable how closely the Church's sacraments and
its sacramental rites parallel the stages of natural human
life. This is a proof of the validity of the sacramental life
of Christian believers. We are born members of the human
family; by Holy Baptism we become members of Christ's
Church and inheritors of the kingdom of heaven. We need
natural strengthening as we assume the duties and responsibilities of adult life; in confirmation we receive the Holy
Spirit to empower us in our Christian profession. We must
be fed continually by natural food if we are to be strong
and healthy; in the Lord's Supper or Holy Communion,
our souls are *strengthened and refreshed* by *the Body and
Blood of Christ, which are spiritually taken and received
by the faithful in the Lord's Supper*. We may marry and
establish a new family; in Holy Matrimony we are blessed
by God and His Church, and thereby strengthened in this
vow and covenant. We go astray and we need assurance
that we are forgiven by those whom we have offended;
in the Church's provision of absolution, we have the assurance of God's forgiveness and love. We are called to various kinds of occupation or profession in order to carry on
the world's work; as Christians we are called to serve God
in our particular vocation and ministry, and those who are
to serve as ordained ministers in Christ's Church are set
apart for their special office. We fall ill, needing medical or
psychiatric assistance so that we may be restored to health;
the Church's rite of unction of the sick provides for us a

162

means by which God's grace can be specially imparted to our soul's health and to the recovery of our body from its ills.

So precise is this correspondence that it is hardly accidental. Those who are of the household of faith believe it to be providential, provided for us by God's care. The sacramental life of the Church is a vital and essential part of Christianity. God cares for His Children, and in His Church He has given us a spiritual home where we grow in grace as we grow in age.

The Resurrection of the Body and the Life Everlasting

IT is often assumed that the Church teaches the immortality of the soul. Actually it teaches something that on the face of it is much more difficult: THE RESURREC-TION OF THE BODY. Now Christian people, in common with non-Christians, normally have found immortality reasonable from the point of view of philosophy and psychology, and the idea of immortality is not in conflict with belief in resurrection—in fact the two well complement each other. But they are not the same.

Immortality implies that there is in man a soul which is innately indestructible, eternity being of its very nature. But resurrection implies that God, by a gift, will raise up and continue in life the whole man, including a medium of expression, *i.e.*, a body. In short, the belief in immortality is conceived in terms of nature: resurrection is to be conceived in terms of grace. Immortality asserts an indestruct-

ible life for the soul; resurrection promises a re-created life
for the whole personality, body and soul. Let us consider
each of these two contrasts.

I

Immortality is of nature, resurrection of grace. Men have
always yearned for the continuity of life, and in virtually
all parts of the world, in almost if not all religions, it is
taught in one form or another. No man's life in this world
is complete; no man here receives complete fulfillment.
This is true whether we consider man's thirst for knowledge (*now we see through a glass, darkly; but then face to
face*)[1] or his thirst for moral vindication (witness the Book
of Job). Completion or fulfillment beyond death seems the
only answer. Men reason thus: all the other universal human yearnings have a response in reality. A man hungers—
and there is food in the world, no matter how difficult it
may be for him to get hold of it. A man has yearnings for
sexual union—and there is in God's order of things a basis
for the fulfillment of this natural urge, namely marriage
and a family. It is difficult to believe that the universal
yearning for continuity of life is not also matched by the
reality of life beyond death.

Furthermore, a man's understanding and vision tran-
scend temporal and spatial limitation. He is capable of
standing over and above the changes and chances of this
mortal life. He binds the past, present, and future together
and so sees their relatedness. Something in him keeps at
work even though the body is asleep. Dreams and the illuminating resolution of problems with which he has gone
to sleep suggest his continuity, regardless of the state of

---

[1] I Corinthians 13:12.

the physical body. Nor is this all. Man's spirit soars to heights above the dimensions of any situation. His spirit at all points defies the rule of mathematics that the total is not greater than the sum of the parts. For him it is greater: there is always more in any human situation than can be counted and measured.

WHY CHRISTIANS BELIEVE IN RESURRECTION

THUS for all these reasons, and others, philosophers have concluded that there is something in man that is above physical process, something which will outlive it, something which is immortal. One could leave it at that, and say that the preponderance of the evidence, or at least the most plausible hypothesis, seems to be on the side of immortality. This is a matter, however, which so affects the character and meaning of life, the priority of its values and the measure of its hopes, that there is a great deal of difference between the significance of a plausible theory and a fact believed as certain.

For a Christian, the life everlasting is a fact believed with certainty. The Christian philosopher and the ordinary layman have shared, each on his own level, with people of many religions, places, and times, a belief in the immortality of the soul. What Christianity does is to transform and limit this expectation. It insists that God alone is the source and sustainer of all life and it proclaims that *he that raised up Christ from the dead shall also quicken* [our] *mortal bodies by his Spirit that dwelleth in us (Romans 8:11)*. The indestructibility of the soul has no necessary place in the Christian teaching of the life to come; the determining fact on man's side is sin which separates us from God: *Who shall deliver me from the body of this death? (Romans 7:24).* If eternal life is merely continuation without an action from God's side to bridge the gulf between Himself and men, who are sinful and inadequate, it would then simply mean projecting sin and inadequacy into all eternity. Obviously that cannot be.

Our confidence in eternal life rests not upon the plausibility of a theory but upon the resurrection of Jesus Christ from the dead. Christ's resurrection and the new life that we even now have in Christ are the guarantee that His promise will be fulfilled: *In my Father's house are many mansions: if it were not so, I would have told you. I go to prepare a place for you. And if I go and prepare a place for you, I will come again and receive you unto myself; that where I am, there ye may be also (St. John 14:2, 3).*[2]

This promise is completely in character with God's love and power, made known supremely in Christ. In the familiar words of the Easter canticle:[3]

Christ being raised from the dead dieth no more; death hath no more dominion over him.

For in that he died, he died unto sin once: but in that he liveth, he liveth unto God.

Likewise reckon ye also yourselves to be dead indeed unto sin, but alive unto God through Jesus Christ our Lord.

Christ is risen from the dead, and become the firstfruits of them that slept.

For since by man came death, by man came also the resurrection of the dead.

[2] See also St. Mark 12:18-27.
[3] Prayer Book, page 163. The portion quoted is Romans 6:9-11 and I Corinthians 15:20-22.

For as in Adam all die, even so in Christ shall all be made alive.

Thus the Church accepts what may be properly believed concerning human immortality based on a rational analysis of the nature of man. But its confidence is grounded more surely in this fact: it rejoices in Christ's glorious resurrection whereby He has *delivered us from the power of our enemy . . . that we may evermore live with him in the joy of his resurrection.*[4]

II

The belief in immortality concerns a life for the soul; faith in resurrection promises a life for the whole personality— body and soul. Christianity is sacramental to the end. Hinduism regards the highest fulfillment beyond this life as a merger of the individual soul with the universal soul or "over-soul," however variously this is phrased. In this way the abiding quality of life is believed to be assured, and the pain, suffering, and sin of this life overcome. But under any such system of thought, terrestrial life is essentially meaningless and valueless. There is no real significance to personal fulfillment for the individual, now or hereafter. Indeed salvation is escape from life as an individual.

The outlook of biblical religion is quite different. The unique quality of each individual is ultimately valuable in God's creative process. Fulfillment means not absorption into some universal substance, but quite the reverse: the heightening of individual qualities and interests. If the individual is absorbed into universality as a drop of water

---

[4] Collect for Easter Day, Prayer Book, page 165.

is absorbed into the sea, such a fulfillment is impossible. It is likewise impossible for the individual as a solitary person. No individual has any meaningful activity, no shape of life, apart from relations with other individuals, apart from the interaction of lives. So while for the Christian everlasting life is individual, not absorption into a universal life, yet it is always social. So we speak of the communion, the fellowship of saints.

In the life to come, just as now, one personality is distinct from another and yet is capable, at the same time, of entering into relations with others, through its appropriate means of expression and communication, its body. A good man may have splendid sentiments in his soul, a fine spirit in his heart, but all this receives significant expression and is known to others only through observable gestures of his hands, sounds coming from his lips, an expression in his eyes, etc. Our familiar word to sum up these means of individual expression is body. Therefore to preserve its understanding of the individual-social (as opposed to universal) character of the life to come, the Christian faith has characteristically used the word *body,* and we use the phrase *resurrection of the body* to affirm the continuity of life in the old body and in the new.

THE NATURE OF THE RESURRECTION BODY

THIS, of course, immediately puts some people off. They think that we are insisting that the physical body known to us in earthly life will at the last trump be magically reconstituted though perhaps long since decayed. But St. Paul writes, *flesh and blood cannot inherit the kingdom of God; neither doth corruption inherit incorruption (I Corinthians 15:50).* Now some Christians have thought that flesh and blood could indeed inherit the Kingdom of God, and for their position we can say this much: God could do this and would, were it the most fitting and appropriate way to fulfill his promises. St. Paul, however, gives us what has become the classical Christian statement. We find it used in the Burial Office in the Prayer Book:

But some man will say, How are the dead raised up? and with what body do they come? Thou foolish one, that which thou sowest is not quickened, except it die: and that which thou sowest, thou sowest not that body that shall be, but bare grain, it may chance of wheat, or of some other grain: but God giveth it a body as it hath pleased him, and to every seed its own body.

All flesh is not the same flesh: but there is one kind of flesh of men, another flesh of beasts, another of fishes, and another of birds. There are also celestial bodies, and bodies terrestrial: but the glory of the celestial is one, and the glory of the terrestrial is another. There is one glory of the sun, and another glory of the moon, and another glory of the stars: for one star differeth from another star in glory. So also is the resurrection of the dead. It is sown in corruption; it is raised in incorruption: it is sown in dishonor; it is raised in glory: it is sown in weakness; it is raised in power: it is sown a natural body; it is raised a spiritual body. There is a natural body, and there is a spiritual body.

And so it is written, The first man Adam was made a living soul; the last Adam was made a quickening spirit. Howbeit that was not first which is spiritual, but that which is natural; and afterward that which is spiritual. The first man is of the earth, earthy: the second man is the Lord from heaven. As is the earthy, such are they also that are earthy: and as is the heavenly, such are they also that are heavenly. And as we have borne the image of the earthy, we shall also bear the image of the heavenly.

Now this I say, brethren, that flesh and blood cannot in-

herit the kingdom of God; neither doth corruption inherit incorruption. Behold, I shew you a mystery; We shall not all sleep, but we shall all be changed, in a moment, in the twinkling of an eye, at the last trump: for the trumpet shall sound, and the dead shall be raised incorruptible, and we shall be changed. For this corruptible must put on incorruption, and this mortal must put on immortality. So when this corruptible shall have put on incorruption, and this mortal shall have put on immortality, then shall be brought to pass the saying that is written, Death is swallowed up in victory. O death, where is thy sting? O grave, where is thy victory? [5]

As St. Paul saw, it is inevitable that men should ask questions of how and what, when they hear the Gospel's assurance that God will bring everything to its divinely willed perfection. St. Paul's answer is illuminating not only as to the manner and nature of the resurrection, but also as to all such questions which men may ask about God's victory in the future. Addressing himself to the specific questions of how God will raise up the dead, and what kind of body they will have, St. Paul argues this way:

First, for the Christian the processes of physical nature are willed and executed by God. They give us, therefore, an analogy of God's working in bringing life through death.

Secondly, a seed planted in the soil does not attain its new plant life except the seed die and decay. St. Paul illustrated this with the wheat grain which through death becomes the new wheat plant.

Thirdly, God gives the new form of life a body appropriate to its new stage of existence, as everywhere one may see how God gives appropriate bodies to essential princi-

---

[5] I Corinthians 15:35-55; and Prayer Book, pages 329-330.

ples: human bodies to human beings, animal bodies appropriate to each animal species, astronomical bodies fitting to the stars and to the moon and to the sun. Even the stars differ in magnitude (glory).

Fourthly, so also is the resurrection of the dead. God's action will re-create those who live in and by God's Spirit, bringing them through death to the perfect life of the Spirit with an appropriate embodiment, a spiritual body. The bodies which we now have, natural bodies, must die and be raised, or must undergo radical change, for *flesh and blood cannot inherit the Kingdom of God.* God, in Christ, has demonstrated Himself trustworthy both in love and power to complete the good work which He has begun in us.

Our human questions as to specific details of when, how, and what are not answered by St. Paul on the level on which they are asked. We are not given information about God's exact method and timing, nor a photograph of the result. But our real question is answered with absolute certainty and clarity. God is consistent, and can be completely trusted to work always and finally as he works in Christ.

What St. Paul wrote to the Corinthians is true to Jesus' word to the Sadducees. When they scoffed at the idea of resurrection, saying that a woman seven times widowed and married would then have seven husbands in the resurrection, Jesus answered, *Ye know not . . . the power of God*—by which we shall be given bodies like the angels, who do not have the sexual relationships which constitute human marriage now (*St. Mark 12:24-25*).

As St. John puts these answers: *Beloved, now are we the sons of God, and it doth not yet appear what we shall be:*

but we know that, when he [Christ] *shall appear, we shall be like him; for we shall see him as he is* (I John 3:2).

In such an attitude we can understand certain affirmations in some Christian pictures of the future without reducing them to photographs which give us concrete details of God's final kingdom. Reasoning that there is an intermediate period between the death of all Christians save the last generation and the final consummation, some have described the departed as grouped in four places. Limbo is for those who had no opportunity to be Christian but who may have the fulfillment of their natural potentialities so that they may enjoy natural bliss. Purgatory is for those who have Christian faith but who, like all of us here, suffer to the degree that they are still imperfect. Paradise is for those whose enjoyment of God is not lessened by any defect in themselves, but it is not the full consummation in which the whole creation participates. This interim period is closed by God's great final perfecting act—the Second Coming of Christ and the new heaven and the new earth. Hell is for those who have shut themselves away from God and God's final community of all His creatures.

Understood as pictures of faith and related to each other as aspects of the Communion of Saints, these teachings may be helpful. Transformed by rationalism and legalism into a supposed literal knowledge, they can be taught in such a way as to contradict God's justice and love as we see them in Christ. What follows is an attempt to state simply the great affirmations of our faith about life after death and the final Consummation in a way that communicates their truth without misrepresenting the kind of certainty which they give.

FIRST of all, see what the Church says about the flesh and the spirit. Sometimes in Christian history an idea has gained currency that things fleshly and things external are bad, and that spiritual realities are the only real good. In its extreme form (found in the most diverse types of Christianity) this notion has led some people to say that celibacy is in itself a higher life than marriage, or that this world has no meaning other than as an anteroom to heaven; it has led other people to say that sex and sensual enjoyment are evil in themselves; it has led some to think that in the realm of worship there can be no holy places, no holy days, no special places or times. Our Church opposes any such notions by its affirmation in every aspect of its teaching, worship, and life, that the world and its joys are good and that particular things are ultimately significant. There is great consistency in the Church's attitude to things bodily, which occupy particular space, and which are different from one another. This tradition takes seriously the word from Genesis (*1:31*), *And God saw every thing that he had made, and, behold, it was very good.*

So we do not conceive of even the life everlasting as disembodied, as universal. As we have seen, it is individual life made socially significant through an external means of experience. We do not regard something as being less spiritual because it is bodily; rather we conceive of it as being more significant spiritually if it is expressed in external, socially communicable terms. In order that holiness may be made manifest, may be made particular and special in its relevance to particular men in particular situations, we affirm that a genuine way to God is by means of holy things,

174

holy places. There are special times and relationships, special places, which provide special opportunities of spiritual meaning. The glory of God's light is seen in its manifold refractions. True, God is present on Sunday at the golf links—although few golfers are aware of him there. But he is specially and more expressively present in the celebration of the Holy Communion when the fellowship of the saints is engaged in participation in holy things in a holy place.

THE CHURCH AND HEAVEN

THIS is why the church building has been called *the gate of heaven*. The action in eucharistic worship, for example, in any humble Christian Church, is not qualitatively unlike heaven. In that service, people who are not by their own rights holy are yet by God's grace engaged in a holy relationship with the Source of holiness and with each other and thus are accounted holy. The offering of each respective life, with all its strength, unique usefulness, weakness, sin, and distress, is accepted and charged with new meaning as it is sent out again into the world. The Holy Communion is the heavenly banquet projected into time. And the same relationship is true, though perhaps less vividly, of the Church's other rites. Thus we can see, or at least sense, the relationship between the communion of saints and participation in holy things, that is, between sanctity and sacraments.

The Episcopal Church, without embarrassment, uses externals as means of grace. There is a good deal of room in the Church, as there always was in its greatest centuries in times past, for differences as to the most suitable details in the expression of the great eternal verities as they touch human life in time. But we all stand committed to the principle that the inward and spiritual is expressible through the outward and visible, and that the latter constitute effectual means to the former. Moreover, we do not view the use of outward and visible forms as a weakness, as less spiritual worship in concession to the flesh; we see it as a strength, in that we thereby affirm the unity of God's creative purpose. For we are expressing in particular instances the great general truth which is the key to the meaning of the whole creation, namely that this is a sacramental universe, that its whole evolving process is an outward and visible sign of the inward and spiritual reality which indwells it, even our God. So we affirm, alike in our worship and in the joy of life: If the outward and visible, the fleshly and bodily, is good enough for God to have created, it is good enough for us to receive and enjoy.

SEPARATION FROM GOD

BUT, of course, outward things may be made ends in themselves. Bodily things may mark the limits of meaning for a man. A man may deliberately reject the claim of a higher meaning and settle for indulgence in things temporal. In short, he may make himself and his own immediate interests the measure of his life. Actually this is the meaning of damnation. Worldliness does not mean the enjoyment of this world; that is permitted Christians, and even enjoined upon them. Worldliness is making this world the limit of one's meaning, the measure of one's values. The worldly man will get what he wants. The world will be the measure of his fulfillment. And that is what HELL is: being barred from what was the highest possibility in store for man, the fulfillment of his life in God and a relationship with others in God as center—a center which gives to each individual his fullest meaning.

HELL IS SELF-WILLED SEPARATION

It is frequently asked, *How could a good God allow men thus to suffer?* The answer is: God has left us free, free either to center our lives in Him or in ourselves. Each one of us is so free that he can devote all that he has or is to the work of God's kingdom here and hereafter, or neglect God's claim upon him and attempt to create a kingdom with himself as king. The first is heaven and the latter is hell. Hell is not a place where men burn forever. It is much worse; it is self-willed separation from Love.

Can such separation from God be final? In principle, yes. By misuse of freedom a man may lose his freedom to respond to God. He may close God out of his life for all eternity. He may rationalize all his faults. He may hide from any judgment upon his life. He may ignore a vision of anything higher. Indeed, he may do this so long that he can virtually no longer hear any voice calling him from the outside. To deny hell in principle would be to deny man's freedom; to confine it to anything short of eternity would be to limit that freedom.

But, when we come to think of how things will in fact work out, we must take into account our experience with God in this life, especially as we have known Him through Jesus Christ. In that experience God never gives up His dealing with an individual soul. In any way that He can reach a man, whether through the insistent voice of conscience, through the influence of others, through the power of tragedy, or through great moments of joy, God continually seeks to get inside the secret places of a man's life and to move him to change his center of life, to get outside of himself and serve the highest. Thus we have ground for the conviction that God does not alter His saving activity toward those who have died, but that, directly and through the fellowship of those that serve Him, He continues to seek those who have closed their lives against Him. It would seem, then, that the door to hell is locked only from the inside.

Whether His persistence and His loving ingenuity and the persuasiveness of the saints will be enough to move all men eventually to turn to God, we do not know. We can hope and pray that the time may come, though perhaps deep into eternity, when there will be no rebel areas, no pockets of resistance. This means that no man may escape the ultimate choice for or against Christ. But it is obvious that many have lived in times and in places and under circumstances which, through no fault of their own, prevented them from knowing Christ. What of them? There is sound scriptural basis for asserting with the historic church that they too will have their opportunity of responding to the love of God made known in Christ. The First Epistle of Peter (*4:6*) records that Christ preached the Gospel to those who had died before His time: . . . *for this cause was the gospel preached also to them that are dead, that they might be judged according to men in the flesh, but live according to God in the spirit.* The great theologians of the Church have understood and taught that such an opportunity for response to God in Christ is required by our belief in God's justice, not to mention our faith in his mercy.

But one thing is certain. God will reign. If we choose to accept His grace and serve Him, God reigns and we with

178

Him. It is good to recall that the original of *whose service is perfect freedom*[6] is *cui servire est regnare* (whom to serve is to reign). If we decline to accept His grace and serve Him, God reigns and without us. As in the Parable of the Wedding Feast (*St. Luke 14:16-24*) when the invited guests would not come, the banquet still went on, so the heavenly banquet will go on. To be absent from it is hell.

The possibility of just such an outcome is not a matter of abstract theology: it is a personal possibility for every man. Since *in the midst of life we are in death*,[7] whether in health or in sickness a man would do well to add to his present prayers the strong cries of petition which are at the opening of what will one day be the service at his grave:

O Lord God most holy, O Lord most mighty, O holy and most merciful Saviour, deliver us not into the bitter pains of eternal death.

Thou knowest, Lord, the secrets of our hearts; shut not thy merciful ears to our prayer; but spare us, Lord most holy, O God most mighty, O holy and merciful Saviour, thou most worthy Judge eternal, suffer us not, at our last hour, for any pains of death, to fall from thee.[8]

THE PILGRIMAGE TO GOD

THERE is on the surface of things an apparent conflict in our expectations. We pray in the Burial Office that the deceased *may go from strength to strength, in the life of perfect service.* We pray also for those who *do now rest from their labors.* Thus the communion of saints is pictured as action and as surcease, as task and as reward, as something yet to be achieved and as something already

---

[6] Collect for Peace, Prayer Book, page 17.
[7] Prayer Book, page 332.
[8] Prayer Book, page 332.

attained. This is a reflection of the fact that in our finite vision we cannot fully express in any one set of words such good things as God has prepared for those who love Him.

Many a saint beholding himself in the burning light will see aspects of his life which require more complete submission to God's reign. And the most profound mystic will find that there is more to know, more to which he can respond in understanding. Even a Paul can say, *Now we see through a glass, darkly; but then face to face (I Corinthians 13:12)*. On the other hand, even the most hardened, self-centered enemy of society is salvageable and perhaps has already, in one or another phase of his character, yielded to higher claims. The most misguided infidel or heretic may be in possession of glimpses of the truth—and whoever knows the truth has had it revealed by God though he know not God's name. This truth and goodness is not *disobedient to the heavenly vision* in its fullness.

To the extent that God is thus enjoyed, to that extent there is peace. To the extent that the blindness of one's past years, the thickness of the defenses which one has erected, still bar one from fellowship with God, to that extent there is struggle and need for the purification of self.

The Prayer Book prays for the soul of one *at the point of departure,* that *whatsoever defilements it may have contracted, through the lusts of the flesh or the wiles of Satan, being purged and done away, it may be presented pure and without spot before thee.*[9] As for those who, in the words of the Prayer Book (page 334), have departed this life *in the true faith of [God's] holy Name* but who have yet to attain their *perfect consummation and bliss,* St. Paul's words afford a vivid picture:

---

[9] Prayer Book, page 317.

For no other foundation can any one lay than that which is laid, which is Jesus Christ. Now if any one builds on the foundation with gold, silver, precious stones, wood, hay, stubble—each man's work will become manifest; for the Day will disclose it, because it will be revealed with fire, and the fire will test what sort of work each one has done. If the work which any man has built on the foundation survives, he will receive a reward. If any man's work is burned up, he will suffer loss, though he himself will be saved, but only as through fire.[10]

Thus there is something still to do. First, there is the task of one's own *continual growth in* [God's] *love and service.*[11] Secondly, because, just as in this life, God reaches us and elicits response not only directly by His Holy Spirit but also through other people, so even those who in their relationship with God are at rest have opportunities for service in relationship to others who are on their way to the completion of their peace. And this is the way it will be as long as there is resistance to God, as long as there is a single place not under His dominion. All the company of heaven will be focused on the strongholds of self-centeredness in the hope that they will yield to the loving persuasiveness of God and His saints, and join in their peace. Such is the fellowship of mutual concern of those who love God.

Yet the enjoyment of God and the glory of the beatific vision is not denied those who are His, simply because there are those who have not submitted to His love. This would be to allow the friends of the devil to play "dog-in-the-manger" with the universe, and would let those who have robbed many of happiness in this life continue that enterprise into eternity. So those who have become His, while

---

[10] I Corinthians 3:11-15. RSV.
[11] Prayer Book, page 75.

never at rest as to any others who have not yet fully turned, are at rest in reference to Him who is their peace. Thus the saints have two kinds of activity: contemplation and service. The enjoyment of the heavenly vision, fellowship with him who is their "heart's desire," the ever-unfolding joy of knowing the heart and mind of God and the glorious beauty of His presence; then, flowing from this content, a discontent that anything, in themselves or in others, stands opposed to Him, and that there is any blindness to this glory.

All this is, of course, mirrored in this present life. The Christian's joy and task here are in the same relationship. Each of us is called to worship and to serve. There need be no conflict between contemplation and action. While there are *diversities of gifts . . . diversities of operations (I Corinthians 12:4, 6)* in the service of God, and thus in actual allotment of time, some may seem to be contemplative and others active, yet in essence every servant of God is called to be both. Those whose lives have such a pattern have a foretaste of heaven. What has been said above about the life to come is true of the Christian life for those yet in their earthly pilgrimage: it is action and surcease, task and reward, something yet to achieve and something already attained.

THE CONSUMMATION

BUT God's revelation carries us even beyond this. It speaks of the end:

> *Every man in his own order: Christ the firstfruits; afterward they that are Christ's at his coming. Then cometh the end, when he shall have delivered up the kingdom to God, even the Father; when he shall have put down all rule, and*

*all authority and power. For he must reign, till he hath put
all enemies under his feet . . . And when all things shall
be subdued unto him, then shall the Son also himself be
subject unto him that put all things under him, that God
may be all in all. (I Corinthians 15:23 ff.)*

This consummation of Christ's reign includes more than
human fulfillment: it involves the whole natural order:

*We know that the whole creation has been groaning in
travail together until now . . .* [waiting] *with eager long-
ing for the revealing of the sons of God: For the creation
was subjected to futility, not of its own will but by the will
of him who subjected it in hope; because the creation itself
will be set free from its bondage to decay and obtain the
glorious liberty of the children of God. (Romans 8:22,
19 ff. RSV.)*

Man in history, in nature, will find his transformed place
in the kingdom in which God is sovereign, for *the kingdoms of this world are become the kingdoms of our Lord,
and of his Christ; and he shall reign forever and ever
(Revelation 11:15).*

Every citizen of such a realm will find his ultimate fulfillment, in the VISION OF GOD. *Now we see through a glass,
darkly; but then face to face (I Corinthians 13:12).*

Amen

THE word *Amen* is not simply a punctuation mark, something indicating the end of a prayer. It means *So be it*. It represents affirmation and response on the part of those saying it. As used at the end of the historic Creeds, it stands for a thought like this, "This is the God to whom we commit ourselves and in whom we put our trust."

Perhaps the most frequently repeated phrase in the Prayer Book is *the Father, the Son, and the Holy Ghost*. At the close of psalm and canticle, the collects for the greater days, and the prayer of consecration in the Holy Communion, churches resound with the praise of the Holy Trinity.

It is often supposed that the Christian Church began with a very simple concept of one God, but that because of the mischief of the theologians who were bent on dogma, the Church now teaches a concept of God which is much more complicated and theoretical; a concept which seems to say that we have three gods rather than one. Actually, however, the doctrine of the Trinity resulted from the efforts of theologians to unify and simplify what were three distinct types of religious experience in which the early Christians shared. A description of the growing experience of God which was characteristic of an early convert will help us to understand the nature of this process.

A young Roman citizen living in the second century of the empire had been noticing that a remarkable change had occurred in the life of a friend of long standing. He was seen with a new set of acquaintances drawn from every level of society, some of them less respectable, some more dignified than those with whom he had previously consorted. About the time the young citizen was ready to ask some questions, he found that his friend was eager to tell him of his new faith. And as a result they both set off to attend one of the meetings of a group of which he was not even told the name. After the friends made their way through an obscure part of the city, they went up to an entrance on a second floor and tapped on the door. The one who answered was greeted with the sign of the fish—the meaning of which was not apparent to the newcomer at the time, but which he later learned meant JESUS CHRIST SON OF GOD SAVIOUR, the first letters of which in Greek formed the word for fish, *ichthus*.[1]

While the visitor did not understand much of what was being said or done in the meeting, before long it became apparent to him that this group of men and women were

---

[1] A transliteration of the Greek may make this clear:
Iesous Jesus
CHristos Christ
THeou God's
Uios Son
Soter Saviour

of one mind, were dominated by an *esprit de corps,* indeed
by a holy *esprit de corps.* This *Holy Spirit* was keeping alive
the small underground movement, giving to its devotees
the courage to face torture rather than deny their new-
found faith, the compulsion to stand firm against the
powers of earth, the will to take the risks involved in commitment to a kingdom higher than the empire while they
yet lived and worked within the empire, and withal a sense
of common concern and affection among *all sorts and conditions of men.* So already the visitor was beginning to
know the fellowship of the Holy Ghost. This was more than
good fellowship. He now knew that he was in touch with
the highest thing that he had ever known, that it was
divine.

This new experience, indeed this Holy Spirit, brought
him back again and again to the group. He began to learn
more and more about one Jesus. He found that these people called themselves Christians because they were Christ's
men. As the figure of Jesus loomed before his own consciousness through the life and the teaching of his new
companions, the time came when he too wanted to become
Christ's man, and to say with the Apostle Thomas, *My
Lord and my God!*

But as he learned more about Jesus he learned about the
Father who had sent Jesus, who created and creates the
world and all that is in it. This was not an entirely new
idea to him; being something of a philosopher, he had
always assumed that behind the gods lay the power of one
God, supreme in immensity, majesty, and creativity. But
now he learned that this God willed to be in personal relationship with His human creatures, that He had acted for
them in Christ to make this relationship possible; and to

the will of that God he responded in faith and commitment.

Like all Christians, he had had an experience of God in three ways.[2] With the rapid rise of Christianity and the speedy absorption of polytheists in the empire and on its borders, it would have been very easy to leave matters there. Indeed, to believe in three gods and to worship three gods would have been quite in character for a religion of that time. The fact is that because they did substitute one God for the many gods of the current religious cults and the State religion, the Jews and Christians in those days were called atheists. But fortunately there were at least two types of persons in the early Christian community who would have found such a situation intolerable. To those of Jewish background monotheism was basic. Through centuries of Jewish worship there had rung the cry *Hear, O Israel: the Lord our God is one Lord.* And the more enlightened Gentiles would have found the assertion of more than one ultimate divine principle philosophically unacceptable and beneath the highest intellectual standards of the day. So the problem was how to hold to the unity of God and to the fullness of their experience of God: God as Father, God as Son, God as Holy Ghost. Thus it is clear that the theologians did not set to work to make a simple faith more complicated; rather they sought to make a unity of what was a complex spiritual experience in the lives of Christian people.

---

[2] The order of experience for him, as for many Christians, is the Holy Ghost, the Son and the Father: first, the Spirit-filled Church, then the Christ whom the Church, through the Spirit, holds before men, and then the Father: *He that hath seen me, hath seen the Father.* Thus we can verify, by tracing its elements back in terms of experience, the phrase in the Creed, *I believe in the Holy Ghost . . . Who proceedeth from the Father and the Son.*

This is an appropriate place, therefore, to say something of the task of the theologian in the Church. People often say, "We want religion and not theology." But we who are Christians are enjoined to worship God with our whole mind as well as with our whole heart. In their service of Christ and His Church, Christian thinkers according to their ability are called upon to devote their gifts of mind to working out the meaning of the Church's experience in response to God's mighty acts and to express that meaning clearly for the benefit of believers in every age. The religious meaning of this enterprise to those with special gifts for undertaking it has been well stated in these words of a contemporary Anglican thinker:

Christian philosophy is an intellectual venture which is necessarily undertaken whenever a man who is endowed with philosophical tastes, gifts, and temperament believes the Christian Faith. I use the word necessarily because such a man cannot believe with the whole of his being unless he believes in a philosophical and intellectual manner. There are indeed diversities of gifts and temperaments, but of all Christians it is true that genuine personal faith must mean the deliberate surrender and dedication of the entire personality to the service of God. The philosophical type of man must thus choose between being a Christian philosopher and not being a Christian at all.[3]

In all centuries many of the most profound Christian minds have dedicated themselves to the consideration of the nature of God as disclosed to man through His self-revelation. In the early centuries it was especially important that the Church have a common understanding of the matter so that in its rapid spread no element of the Chris-

---

[3] J. V. Langmead Casserley, *The Christian in Philosophy* (1949), page 11.

tian experience of God would be denied or minimized to the impoverishment of the Church and of the Christian life of its members, present and to come.

The classic formulation of the doctrine of the Trinity was developed in the councils of the fourth and fifth centuries in the attempt to work out the doctrines of Christ and the Holy Spirit.[4] Naturally the words and concepts which were used by the councils and the theologians of this period reflect the thought-forms customary in the intelligent discourse of the day. Yet what was being formulated was a description of the eternal nature of Deity as revealed by the mighty acts of God in history. Therefore we as Christians of the twentieth century are bound by what was being expressed but not by the particular mode of expression of those centuries, or for that matter, of any century. But in our own explanations in the language and thought-forms of our day, we necessarily use the classical formulations as our point of departure and standard of orthodoxy. We do so for at least three reasons:

First, at that time the Catholic Church was more of a visible unity; hence it was possible to gain for a given form of words a *consensus fidelium* (consent of the faithful) throughout most of the Christian world.

Secondly, the Church has continued to use these words, and thus they form a link between Christian groups which are now separated. In the present divided state of Christendom it would be impossible to find substitutes which could receive general acceptance.

Thirdly, the old words have gathered about them a vast amount of interpretation through the centuries, as well as hallowed liturgical and devotional associations. All this

---

[4] See Chapters VI, VIII; also *Chapters in Church History,* pages 31-38.

would be largely lost to subsequent ages if the traditional words were allowed to lose their living function in the life of the Church. Therefore it is the task of the Church in this and in every age to pass on these revered carriers of divine truth, and then to translate them into concepts which make them real in the personal religion of contemporary Churchmen.

So in regard to the formulation of the doctrine of the Trinity, we must distinguish what was being communicated from the way the Church has normatively communicated it. As we have already seen, what was being expressed is the living experience of the active power of God in three distinct relationships, and the conviction that in each of these experiences the Christian is in touch with God himself, a God who is one, not three.

We believe that when one knows Christ he is in touch with nothing less than the true God. Furthermore, that when one is moved by the Spirit one is moved by nothing less than the true God.

That Christ and the Holy Spirit are not passing phases of God's activity, not just ways in which He appears at particular times, but that they are permanent, indeed eternal, expressions of His being.

That the relationships of supreme love, which, for example, we see manifested in Christ's love of the Father, are permanent interpersonal relationships in God. That what we have known in our threefold experience of God is not illusion, but has its source in the nature of God Himself and that this nature has never changed and never will change.

As to the form of words traditionally used to express these convictions, we can best appreciate them if we realize that historically speaking each phrase was hammered out to prevent a distortion of the full truth by various plausible half-truths. Against those who would define the nature of God in such a way as to make Father, Son, and Holy Ghost mere temporal modes of God's action (*modalism*) the Church has affirmed: *Three persons.*[5] Against those who would define the nature of God in such a way as to make Father, Son, and Holy Ghost virtually three Gods (*tritheism*) the Church has affirmed: *The Godhead of the Father, of the Son, and of the Holy Ghost is all one.* Against those who would define the Son or the Holy Ghost as derivative powers acting for God (*subordinationism*) the Church has affirmed *the glory equal, the majesty co-eternal.*

The Church's definitions are based on the conviction that behind our triune experience is triune Reality. And this in turn is based on two fundamental assumptions: that there is a real correspondence between Reality and our human experience; and, more than that, that God is Truth and wills to reveal Himself to us truly. Therefore, though what we affirm about the Trinity is the summary of our experience of Him, yet it is also a reflection of what He is. And this He has been from all eternity and always shall be. Love, fellowship, and spiritual fulfillment, which depend on interpersonal relationships, always have been God's. Their realization did not depend upon the arrival in the universe of other personal beings.

Because the Church has labored to preserve the full understanding of God in the doctrine of the Holy Trinity,

---

[5] The meaning of person in theological language is not to be confused with our modern use of the term personality. It implies, rather, a distinct and eternal expression of God's being corresponding to each of the ways in which God acts in the world: Father, Son, and Holy Ghost.

individual Christians in all ages have been able to recapitulate the experience of the Christians of the earliest centuries and to come into living touch with the Father, the Son, and the Holy Ghost. Truly, in the words of the ancient *Quicunque vult,*[6] "This is the Catholic faith: that we worship Godhead in Trinity and Trinity in Unity."

Thus the devout believer who has little or no familiarity with the proceedings of the Councils of Nicaea and Chalcedon has been able to say with personal conviction, and conviction which affirms the Trinity and the Unity, the words of the Catechism and Office of Instruction:

First, I learn to believe in God the Father, who hath made me, and all the world.

Secondly, in God the Son, who hath redeemed me, and all mankind.

Thirdly, in God the Holy Ghost, who sanctifieth me, and all the people of God.

And this Holy Trinity, One God, I praise and magnify, saying,

Glory be to the Father, and to the Son, and to the Holy Ghost;

As it was in the begining, is now, and ever shall be, world without end. Amen.

---

[6] This is the creed often attributed to St. Athanasius, but probably dating from the century after his death. It is a part of the liturgy of the Church of England and will be found in the English Prayer Book, pages 67-70.

Books for Reference

THE selection of books which appears below
is intended to assist those who wish to read further concerning the Faith of the Church. Those volumes which are written
by members of the Anglican Communion, that is, the Episcopal Church and its sister Churches, are marked by an as-
terisk in all sections but that one headed *General*. In the
general category, all but one or two of the writers are Anglicans.

Books which are fairly easy to read, or which can be read
with the use of any ordinary dictionary, are here labeled
POPULAR. Those which presuppose theological or philosophical
training are listed as MORE ADVANCED.

The authors do not necessarily agree with everything in the
books that appear in this bibliography. Titles are included
because they represent a point of view, or state a position,
which is held within the Episcopal Church; or because they
will enable the reader to think more profoundly on the topic
in question. It has been the policy to avoid reference to specific
chapters on specific subjects, excepting in a very few instances,
since those who wish to pursue their study of the Church's
faith will doubtless wish to read a number of books straight
through, rather than carry on their reading by small snippets
of a few pages here and there.

Finally, the list is limited to books which are in print or
are easily available from libraries of religious literature. This
means that some older volumes must necessarily be omitted.
In all but a few instances the books listed were originally pub-
lished within the last twenty-five years.

GENERAL

POPULAR

The Case for Christianity by C. S. Lewis (New York: Macmillan. 1945). A simple and effective argument for the Christian faith; very direct and readable.

We Believe by Angus Dun (Milwaukee: Morehouse. 1934). The Bishop of Washington has written a straightforward explanation of the Creed, understandable by any layman.

The Christian Way in a Modern World by W. Norman Pittenger (Chicago: Wilcox Follett. 1946). A statement of the Christian faith, designed for college students or graduates, covering most aspects of the belief, worship, and life of Christians as Episcopalians see them.

No Faith of My Own by Langmead Casserley (New York: Longmans, Green. 1950). A stimulating apologetic for Christianity by a brilliant English sociologist converted to the Faith from rationalism.

Christian Faith and Practice by Leonard Hodgson (New York: Scribners. 1951).
Christian Belief by A. R. Vidler (New York: Scribners. 1950). Two series of lectures to university audiences, the former at Oxford, the latter at Cambridge. Excellent for general reading. An earlier book by Dr. Vidler, *Plain Man's Guide to Christianity* (London: Heinemann. 1936), will also be found valuable.

The Gospel and Modern Thought by Alan Richardson (New York: Oxford. 1950). An admirable apologetic for Christianity with special attention to the scientific mentality of our time. Slightly more advanced than the books mentioned above.

The Religion of the Prayer Book by Powel M. Dawley and Walden Pell (New York: Morehouse-Gorham. 1946). A survey of the teaching of the American Book of Common Prayer drawing out its practical implications for the layman.

The School of Charity by Evelyn Underhill (New York: Longmans, Green. 1934). A beautifully written devotional commentary on the Church's Creed.

194

The Framework of Faith by Leslie Simmonds (New York: Longmans, Green. 1939). A somewhat more advanced but still readable discussion of the presuppositions and implications of Christian belief. Good for students.

Christian Doctrine by J. S. Whale (New York: Macmillan. 1948). The only volume in this list not by an Anglican, Dr. Whale's book is widely used in the Episcopal Church; it is one of the finest careful surveys of Christian belief available today. Somewhat advanced.

MORE ADVANCED

Nature, Man and God by William Temple (London: Macmillan. 1934). A standard work, often called the best contemporary apologetic for the Christian conception of God and the Christian view of life.

The Faith of a Moralist by A. E. Taylor (London: Macmillan. 1930). A philosophical defense of the Christian faith; the second section is particularly valuable for its brilliant statement of the Anglican position on authority, institutions, sacraments, etc.

Theological Outlines by F. J. Hall, edited by F. H. Hallock (New York: Morehouse-Gorham. 1933). A shorter version of the many-volumed work on dogmatic theology for which Dr. Hall won great fame. This is the standard reference work for those who wish to check on the traditional Christian view on any theological matter.

Doctrines of the Creed by Oliver C. Quick (New York: Scribners. 1938). More modern in approach than Hall, Canon Quick surveys the Creeds and discusses their teaching in philosophical idiom.

The Christian Faith by C. B. Moss (New York: Morehouse-Gorham. 1944). This recent book covers the same ground as Hall and Quick, but with less philosophical reasoning than Quick and more discursively than Hall.

The Christian Faith edited by W. R. Matthews (London: Eyre Spottiswoode. 1936). A series of essays on the major doctrines of the Church by distinguished contemporary English theologians.

195

Reconstruction of Belief by Charles Gore (New York: Scribners. 1923). This massive volume covers the entire range of Christian belief, with attention to many related aspects of modern thought and with special attention to the problems of educated inquirers.

Dogmatics in Outline by Karl Barth (New York: Philosophical Library. 1950). This is the only book in this group by a non-Episcopalian. Barth is one of the most important theologians of our time; in this small book he summarizes his teachings on the Creed. Valuable for its strong Biblical emphasis.

Outline of Christian Dogma by Darwell Stone (London: Longmans, Green. 1907). A conservative theology, yet keenly aware of newer ideas. Used in some of our seminaries as a convenient summary of the Faith.

ANGLICAN THEOLOGY: Historical

Anglicanism edited by Paul Elmer More and Frank Leslie Cross (New York: Morehouse-Gorham. 1935). A magnificent selection of characteristic writings of the so-called Caroline divines, from Hooker to Ken, with a preface on the spirit of Anglicanism by Dr. More. The best introduction to the historical genius of Anglicanism.

The Ecclesiastical Polity by Richard Hooker. The "judicious Hooker" is often called "the father of Anglican theology." His *Ecclesiastical Polity,* although written against the background of Elizabethan controversy, is still highly readable. A shortened version has been prepared by John S. Marshall (Sewanee: University of the South Press. 1948).

Three volumes which give different approaches to the common faith of the Church have acquired the status of Anglican classics; all have appeared within the last seventy-five years:

Lux Mundi edited by Charles Gore (London: John Murray. 1890).

Foundations edited by B. H. Streeter (London: Macmillan. 1922).

196

Essays Catholic and Critical edited by E. Gordon Selwyn (New York: Macmillan. 1927).

A fourth volume, prepared by a special commission appointed in England, is often cited in connection with the various approaches to the faith found in the Anglican Communion:

Doctrine in the Church of England. Report of the Commission on Doctrine appointed by the Archbishops of Canterbury and York, 1922 (New York: Macmillan. 1938).

CHAPTER I: THE GOSPEL

POPULAR

The Man Christ Jesus (Chicago: Willett, Clark. 1941) and *Christ the Lord* (Chicago: Willett, Clark. 1945) by John Knox. Two excellent books for the layman. To be read with Knox's *The Meaning of Christ* (see the suggestions for Chapter VI).

* *Scripture and Faith* by A. G. Hebert (London: Catholic Literature Association. 1948). Does for the layman what Fr. Hebert has done for the scholar in his book mentioned below.

MORE ADVANCED

The Apostolic Preaching by C. Harold Dodd (London: Holder and Stoughton. 1936). A brief and readable summary of the New Testament evidence.

* *An Introduction to New Testament Thought* by F. C. Grant (Nashville: Abingdon-Cokesbury. 1950). The best thorough treatment of the beginnings of Christian theology in New Testament times and writings.

* *The Bible from Within* by A. G. Hebert (New York: Oxford. 1950). A discussion of the way in which the entire scriptural record converges on the gospel of redemption in Christ.

CHAPTER II: THE NATURE OF BELIEF

POPULAR

* *Christianity and the Modern World View* by H. A. Hodges (New York: Macmillan. 1950). A brief and clear exposition of what is often posed as an issue between Christian faith and secularist reason, but which is in fact the issue of a more adequate faith *vs.* a less adequate one.

* *Miracles* by C. S. Lewis (New York: Macmillan. 1947). Primarily concerned with the Christian attitude toward the miraculous, this book covers many other important aspects of the mode of belief.

* *The Gospel and Modern Thought* by Alan Richardson (New York: Oxford. 1950). A fine analysis of the relationship of science and religion, revelation and miracle, with a brief survey of the whole of Christian doctrine.

MORE ADVANCED

Our Knowledge of God by John Baillie (New York: Scribners. 1939). A careful analysis of the process of believing in God, with attention to various religious and philosophical positions, historic and contemporary.

* *Christian Apologetics* by Alan Richardson (London: S.C.M. 1947). The most thorough current treatment of the relation of theology to the scientific disciplines, and of the validity of approaches to belief through miracle, prophecy, the Bible, revelation, and reason.

FOR EVEN MORE ADVANCED READERS

Philosophical Understanding and Religious Truth by Erich Frank (New York: Oxford. 1945).

The Meaning of Revelation by H. Richard Niebuhr (New York: Scribners. 1939).

The Primacy of Faith by Richard Kroner (New York: Macmillan. 1943).

CHAPTER III: GOD

THE doctrine of God is thoroughly discussed in the several books listed under the General heading; reference should also be made to G. B. Caird, *The Truth of the Gospel* (New York: Oxford. 1950), for a good treatment of this question.

POPULAR

God by Walter Horton (New York: Association Press. 1937). An excellent brief statement of the Christian teaching about God.

Prayer in a World of Science by W. A. Brown (New York: Scribners. 1927). A popular treatment of the subject, readable by laymen.

The Christian Answer to the Problem of Evil by J. S. Whale (New York: The Abingdon Press. 1936). Very simple and readable.

* *The Problem of Pain* by C. S. Lewis (New York: Macmillan. 1943). In his usual brilliant style, Lewis discusses this problem, throwing light incidentally on many other matters of Christian concern.

MORE ADVANCED

* *God in Christian Thought and Experience* by W. R. Matthews (London: Nisbet. 1930). A discussion of the problems and implications in the Christian doctrine of God by the dean of St. Paul's Cathedral, London.

* *He Who Is* by E. L. Mascall (New York: Longmans, Green. 1943). An argument for and statement of the traditional Christian conception of God, with special attention to philosophical questions.

* *God and Reality* by M. Bowyer Stewart (New York: Longmans, Green. 1926). Particularly good for its description of the idea of the transcendence, concomitance, and immanence of God.

* *God of the Living* by R. H. L. Slater (New York: Scribners. 1939). A somewhat simpler statement of the same ideas as found in Matthews' book.

The World and God by H. H. Farmer (New York: Harpers. 1936). A careful treatment of the problem of miracle, providence, and prayer in a world of science.

CHAPTER IV: MAN

The Nature and Destiny of Man by Reinhold Niebuhr (New York: Scribners. 1943). The most definitive work of our time on the predicament of contemporary man in the light of the Christian understanding of man and history.

What Is Man? by Robert L. Calhoun (New York: Association Press. 1939). A briefer exposition of the doctrine of man in terms of contemporary relevance.

Christian Understanding of Man (New York: Oxford. 1937). A series of papers prepared by theologians of various Christian Churches in connection with the Oxford Conference on Church, Community, and State.

Psychotherapy and a Christian View of Man by David E. Roberts (New York: Scribners. 1950). An exposition of certain aspects of depth psychology in their relation to the Christian doctrine of man, thus providing also a relevant reinterpretation of the latter.

Man in Revolt by Emil Brunner (New York: Scribners. 1939). A brilliant and carefully analyzed treatment informed by the new Protestant orthodoxy.

* *Down Peacock's Feathers* by D. R. Davies (New York: Macmillan. 1946). With explicit reference to the current scene (as of the time of writing), this work takes the form of a commentary on the General Confession.

True Humanism by Jacques Maritain (New York: Scribners. 1938). An analysis by a contemporary Roman Catholic scholar who sees man without the religious dimension as less than human.

* *Idea of the Fall and Original Sin* by Norman Powell Williams (New York: Longmans, Green. 1927). An historical and analytical treatment of these two basic doctrines.

CHAPTER V: SALVATION

* *The Christian Doctrine of Grace* by Oscar Hardman (New York: Macmillan. 1947). An historical and analytical treatment of the meaning of grace.

* *Atonement and Personality* by R. C. Moberly (New York: Longmans, Green. 1901. First American edition. London: John Murray. 1932. Eleventh English edition). A study of man's redemption in relationship to his creation in the image of God.

The World's Ransom by E. R. Micklem (London: S.C.M. 1946). A series of meditative analyses of various aspects of our redemption in Christ.

* *Instructions on the Atonement* by Paul B. Bull (New York: Longmans, Green. 1901). A little book on the work of Christ which combines doctrinal analysis with persuasive homily.

Jesus and His Sacrifice by Vincent Taylor (London: Macmillan. 1937). The most definitive study of the meaning of the Atonement in the New Testament.

* *The Doctrine of the Atonement* by Leonard Hodgson (New York: Scribners. 1951). A scholarly study by a distinguished Anglican theologian.

* *The Gospel of the New World* by Oliver Quick (London: Nisbet. 1944). Beginning with the problem of evil and ending with the Christian view of resurrection, this book covers briefly the history of the doctrine of the Atonement.

The Doctrine of Our Redemption by Nathaniel Micklem (Nashville: Abingdon-Cokesbury. 1948). Another history of the doctrine with more detailed treatment of the main motifs which emerge during the Christian centuries up through the Reformation period.

The Doctrine of the Work of Christ by Sidney Cave (Nashville: Abingdon-Cokesbury. 1937). A still more detailed history of the doctrine, for more advanced readers.

* *Atonement in History and Life* a symposium edited by L. W. Grensted (New York: Macmillan. 1929).

* *The Doctrine of the Atonement* by J. K. Mozley (New York: Scribners. 1916).

CHAPTER VI: CHRIST

POPULAR

Our Eternal Contemporary by Walter Marshall Horton (New York: Harpers. 1942). A survey, readable by laymen, of recent thought about the meaning of Christ in theological circles.

* *And Was Made Man* by Leonard Hodgson (New York: Longmans, Green. 1928). Somewhat stiff reading but eminently rewarding; a scholarly book with great religious depth and devotional suggestion.

* *The God-Man* by E. L. Mascall (London: Dacre Press. 1940). A good brief statement of the orthodox Christology in simple style.

* *The Christ of God* by Henry Balmforth (London: S.C.M. 1938). Another statement, intended for laymen.

The Meaning of Christ by John Knox (New York: Scribners. 1947). A summary of the theological implications of the New Testament picture of Christ, written for general reading.

MORE ADVANCED

God Was in Christ by Donald M. Baillie (New York: Scribners. 1948). Especially good for his use of the concept of paradox in relation to Christology.

* *Christ the Truth* by William Temple (London: Macmillan. 1934). A discussion of Christology in modern terms with special reference to philosophical problems.

* *The Incarnate Lord* by L. S. Thornton (London: Longmans, Green. 1928). A massive work, restating the doctrine of Christ in terms of modern organismic philosophy.

* *The Divinity of Jesus Christ* by J. M. Creed (Cambridge University Press. 1938). An excellent summary of Christological thought during the past century.

* *Christ the Word* by Paul Elmer More (Princeton University Press. 1927).

* *Christ and Christian Faith* by W. Norman Pittenger (New York: Round Table Press. 1941). A statement of the Incarnation written in defense of Chalcedonian Christology but with attention to New Testament criticism.

Specifically on the Virgin Birth are these two works:

* *The Virgin Birth* by Douglas Edwards (London: Faber and Faber. 1943).

The Virgin Birth by Vincent Taylor (Oxford: Clarendon Press. 1920).

CHAPTER VII: "HE ROSE . . . HE ASCENDED . . . HE SHALL COME TO JUDGE . . ."

Very little has been written specifically on this subject; chapters may be found in the volumes listed under the heading General. See also:

* *The Resurrection of Christ* by A. M. Ramsey (London: Centenary Press. 1946). A careful analysis in small compass of the relevant biblical material.

Christ and Time by Oscar Cullmann (Philadelphia: Westminster. 1950). A difficult but rewarding treatment of the problem of time and eternity in relation to God's act of redemption in Christ.

* *Civilization on Trial* by Arnold Toynbee (New York: Oxford. 1948) Chapters XIII, XIV. Essays by the distinguished philosopher of history on the relation of this world to the Kingdom of God.

Other treatments of the Christian understanding of history:

Faith and History by Reinhold Niebuhr (New York: Scribners. 1949).

Christianity and History by Herbert Butterfield (New York: Scribners. 1950).

Christian Understanding of History by E. C. Rust (London: Lutterworth Press. 1947).

CHAPTER VIII: THE HOLY SPIRIT

VERY little has been written specifically on this subject; chapters may be found in the volumes listed under the heading General. See also:

* *Creator Spirit* by C. E. Raven (London: M. Hopkinson. 1927). For advanced readers.

* *The Holy Spirit in the Life of Today* by F. W. Dillistone (Philadephia: Westminster Press. 1947). For general reading.

CHAPTER IX: THE CHURCH

POPULAR

* *The Church of God* by D. M. McKinnon (London: Dacre Press. 1940). A discussion of the nature of the Church, with a call to Christian action that "the Church may be the Church."

* *The Church of God* by F. J. Taylor (London: Canterbury Press. 1946). Similar to the above, but from a more evangelical point of view.

* *The Church* by J. W. C. Wand (New York: Morehouse-Gorham. 1948). Another treatment like those above, but in this instance more Catholic in approach.

* *The Beloved Community* by Roger Lloyd (New York: Macmillan. 1937). The Church as providing for men that social life which guarantees their true personality in God.

* *The Living Temple* by William H. Dunphy (New York: Morehouse-Gorham. 1933). The meaning of the Church is discussed with special attention to the rich teaching about its nature found in Eastern Orthodox liturgy and in the ancient Fathers.

The classical Anglican treatment of the nature of the Christian ministry is * *Ministerial Priesthood* by R. C. Moberly (London: Murray. 1897) which is for advanced readers. For a statement of the Anglican position, as against Roman Catholic claims, see * *The Church of Rome: A Dissuasive* by R. H. Hanson and Reginald Fuller (London: S.C.M. 1949). A consideration of the Anglican view in relation to other communions, especially Protestant, will be found in * *The Claims of the Church of England* by Cyril Garbett (London: Hodder and Stoughton. 1947).

MORE ADVANCED

* *The Form of the Church* by A. G. Hebert (London: Faber and Faber. 1944). A discussion of the nature and functions of the Church.

* *The Gospel and the Catholic Church* by A. M. Ramsey (New York: Macmillan. 1944). An excellent summary of the relations between Scripture and Church tradition.

* *The Coming Great Church* by Theodore O. Wedel (New York: Macmillan. 1945). A treatment which gives special attention to questions of Christian reunion.

* *His Body the Church* by W. Norman Pittenger (New York: Morehouse-Gorham. 1945). A systematic treatment of the meaning of the Church in relation to the doctrine of the Incarnation.

* *Christ, the Christian and the Church* by E. L. Mascall (New York: Longmans, Green. 1946). Concerned to emphasize especially the fact of incorporation of the believer into the living Body of Christ.

* *Common Life in the Body of Christ* by L. S. Thornton (London: Dacre Press. 1942). A deeply scriptural study of the Church and the Christian life, influenced by the organic philosophy stated in the author's *Incarnate Lord*.

CHAPTER X: THE SACRAMENTS

POPULAR

* *The Worshipping Community* by H. C. L. Heywood (Milwaukee: Morehouse. 1938). A popular treatment of the faith in the light of sacramental worship.

* *The Oxford American Prayer Book Commentary* by Massey Shepherd (New York: Oxford University Press. 1950). Covers all the sacraments and sacramental ordinances for which the Prayer Book provides, with brief exposition of each and with an account of their historical development.

MORE ADVANCED

* *The Christian Sacraments* by Oliver C. Quick (New York: Harpers. 1927). The best thorough discussion of the sacramental idea and the particular sacraments.

* *Liturgy and Society* by A. G. Hebert (London: Faber and Faber. 1935). A very influential study of the social implications of the Christian sacramental position.

* *The Christian Sacrifice* by W. Norman Pittenger (New York: Oxford University Press. 1951). A theological discussion of the Eucharist and its relation to the nature of the Church.

Eucharistic Faith and Practice—Evangelical and Catholic by Yngve Brilioth (New York: Macmillan. 1931). A careful work by the Archbishop of Upsala appraising the several eucharistic traditions.

On the theological problems connected with Confirmation, advanced readers may wish to examine * *The Theology of Christian Initiation,* the report of a theological commission appointed by the Archbishops of Canterbury and York to advise on the relations between Baptism, Confirmation, and Holy Communion (London: S.P.C.K. 1948), and * *The Theology of Confirmation in Relation to Baptism* by Dom Gregory Dix (London: Dacre Press. 1946).

CHAPTER XI: ETERNAL LIFE

And the Life Everlasting by John Baillie (New York: Scribners. 1933). An inspiring analysis of the Christian faith about the life to come.

* *If Man Die* by Wilbur C. Bell (London: Scribners. 1934). A popular treatment of the considerations which move men to belief in eternal life.

* *Resurrection of the Body* by Oscar Hardman (New York: Macmillan. 1934). A scholarly treatment of the doctrine which is to be distinguished from "immortality."

* *In the End, God* by J. A. T. Robinson (London: James Clarke. 1951). An excellent discussion of the meaning of Christian eschatology.

* *The Great Divorce* by C. S. Lewis (New York: Macmillan. 1946). A suggestive treatment of the life to come in the form of an allegorical tale.

This Life and the Next by P. T. Forsyth (London: Macmillan. 1918).

* *Christianity and Immortality* by Vernon Storr (New York: Longmans, Green. 1918).

These books also provide convincing apologetic for the Christian hope:

* *Can We Still Believe in Immortality?* by Frederick C. Grant (Louisville: Cloister Press. 1944).

* *The Christian Hope of Immortality* by A. E. Taylor (New York: Macmillan. 1947).

CHAPTER XII: THE TRINITY

* *Beyond Personality* by C. S. Lewis (New York: Macmillan. 1945). A forthright apologetic for the Christian doctrine of God in three persons.

* *The Trinity and Christian Devotion* by Charles Lowry (New York: Harpers. 1946). A more analytical treatment with special reference to the bearing of the doctrine of the Trinity on the Christian life of prayer and worship.

* *Mind of the Maker* by Dorothy L. Sayers (New York: Harcourt Brace. 1942). A bold and imaginative treatment of the doctrine, making free use of such analogies as an author's experience of creativity.

* *Doctrine of the Trinity* by Leonard Hodgson (New York: Scribners. 1944). A definitive treatment firmly grounded in the Christian doctrine of Revelation.

* *Essays on the Trinity and Incarnation* edited by A. E. J. Rawlinson (London: Longmans, Green. 1928). A collection of monographs representing the best English scholarship.

Biblical References

ABOUT THE AUTHORS

THE VERY REV. JAMES A. PIKE, J.S.D., D.D., is Dean of the Cathedral of St. John the Divine and Adjunct Professor of Religion, Columbia University, where he served as Chaplain and head of the Department of Religion before coming to the Cathedral. A graduate of the University of Southern California (A.B., LL.B.) he was Sterling Fellow at the Yale Law School and received the degree of Doctor of the Science of Law there in 1938. For four years he was an attorney with the Securities Exchange Commission in Washington and on the faculty of the George Washington University Law School. During World War II Dean Pike served as a line officer in the Navy. A former Roman Catholic, he was ordained deacon in 1944 and attended the Virginia, General and Union Theological Seminaries, graduating from the latter, meanwhile having served as a Fellow and Tutor at General, of which seminary he is now a Trustee. Before serving at Columbia Dr. Pike was rector of Christ Church, Poughkeepsie, New York, and in charge of student work at Vassar College. He is author of a number of law books and of *Beyond Anxiety, If You Marry Outside Your Faith,* and *Doing the Truth,* and co-author of *Roadblocks to Faith and Church, Politics and Society.* Dr. Pike is a Fellow of the National Council of Religion in Higher Education and is a member of the Joint Department of Religious Liberty of the National Council of Churches. He is president of the Standing Committee of the Diocese of New York.

THE REV. W. NORMAN PITTENGER, S.T.D., is Professor of Apologetics at the General Theological Seminary. He has been on the teaching staff of the seminary since his graduation from that institution in 1936, and has served as Lecturer in Religion at Columbia University where he did graduate work. He also studied at Union Theological Seminary. He is a former vice president of the Church Congress, former president of the American Theological Society, member of the Study Commission of the World Council of Churches on The Ethical Task of the Church, and consultant to the Commission on the Church and Social Problems of the National Council of Churches of Christ in America. He is the author of a number of theological volumes, including *Christ and Christian Faith: A Study of the Incarnation,* and *His Body the Church;* and also of several popular statements of Christianity, among them *The Christian Way in a Modern World* and *A Living Faith for Living Men.* His most recent books are *The Historic Faith and a Changing World, The Christian Sacrifice, Christ in the Haunted Wood, The Christian View of Sexual Behavior, Christian Affirmations,* and *Theology and Reality.*

THE REV. STANLEY BROWN-SERMAN, D.D., formerly Dean and Professor of New Testament Language and Literature at the Protestant Episcopal Theological Seminary in Virginia.

THE REV. POWEL MILLS DAWLEY, PH.D., Professor of Ecclesiastical History at the General Theological Seminary and author of Volume II and Volume VI in THE CHURCH TEACHING series, *Chapter in Church History* and *The Episcopal Church and Its Work*.

THE REV. ROBERT CLAUDE DENTAN, PH.D., Professor of Old Testament Literature and Interpretation at the General Theological Seminary and author of the Volume I in THE CHURCH'S TEACHING series, *The Holy Scriptures*.

THE REV. FREDERICK W. DILLISTONE, D.D., Canon and Chancellor at Liverpool Cathedral, England.

THE REV. JOHN HEUSS, D.D., formerly Director, The Department of Christian Education of The National Council and now rector of Trinity Church, New York City.

THE RT. REV. ARTHUR C. LICHTENBERGER, D.D., Bishop of Missouri and former professor at the General Theological Seminary.

THE REV. ALBERT T. MOLLEGEN, D.D., Professor of Christian Ethics at the Protestant Episcopal Theological Seminary in Virginia.

THE REV. C. KILMER MYERS, Vicar of St. Augustine's Chapel, Trinity Parish, New York.

THE REV. FREDERICK Q. SHAFER, Associated Professor of Christian Ethics and Philosophy at the Associated Colleges at Claremont, California.

THE REV. MASSEY H. SHEPHERD, JR., PH.D., Professor of Liturgics at the Church Divinity School of the Pacific and author of Volume IV in THE CHURCH'S TEACHING series, *The Worship of the Church*.

THE REV. CHARLES W. F. SMITH, D.D., Professor of New Testament at Episcopal Theological School.

THE REV. VESPER O. WARD, D.D., Professor of Christian Education and Homiletics at the School of Theology, the University of the South.

THE REV. THEODORE O. WEDEL, PH.D., Warden of the College of Preachers, Washington, D. C.

Index

6-356-C-10

DATE DUE